PATRICK H. PERRINE

Sales and Scale

*The Entrepreneur's Blueprint for Mastering Marketing
and Achieving Explosive Growth*

DEDICATION

To the trailblazing marketers and unwavering entrepreneurs who navigate the ever-changing seas of commerce with grace and tenacity: May this volume serve as your compass, steering you toward unbound success and growth in the art of sales and marketing.

Warmly,
Patrick

"Branding is the process of connecting good strategy with good creativity."

— MARTY NEUMEIER

Contents

Preface

Welcome to 'Sales and Scale: The Entrepreneur's Blueprint for Mastering Marketing and Achieving Explosive Growth,' your navigational beacon through the dynamic and often turbulent waters of modern marketing and sales. As the sixth volume in the 'Be A Unicorn' series, this book builds directly upon the insights from Step 6 of 'Unicorn Rising,' diving deeper into the critical aspects of marketing and sales that fuel the growth and success of any entrepreneurial venture.

In today's rapidly changing business environment, understanding and leveraging the power of marketing and sales are more crucial than ever. 'Sales and Scale' is designed to be both a comprehensive guide and a practical workbook, offering you advanced strategies, real-life examples, and actionable advice to effectively promote your products or services and achieve your business goals.

From deciphering the complexities of your target market to mastering the art of digital and traditional marketing channels, this volume serves as your roadmap to navigating the multi-faceted world of marketing and sales. Each chapter is crafted to provide you with a deeper understanding of a specific aspect of marketing or sales, accompanied by practical exercises and templates that you can apply directly to your business.

As we explore the symbiotic relationship between marketing and sales, you'll learn how these essential components intertwine to create a formidable strategy that can propel your business to new heights. Whether you're laying the foundations of your startup or seeking to enhance the marketing prowess of your established business, 'Sales and Scale' offers the insights and tools necessary to navigate today's competitive landscape successfully.

'Sales and Scale' is more than just a book; it's a part of a larger journey within the 'Be A Unicorn' series, designed to accompany you as you scale the peaks of entrepreneurial achievement. By integrating the teachings from this volume with the knowledge acquired in previous installments, you'll be equipped to turn your entrepreneurial aspirations into tangible market successes.

Embark on this journey with 'Sales and Scale,' and unlock the secrets to mastering marketing and sales. Embrace the strategies within to drive growth, create brand awareness, and achieve explosive growth. Let's begin with Chapter 1: Understanding Your Target Market, laying the groundwork for a marketing strategy that resonates, engages, and converts.

Prepare to transform your entrepreneurial vision into a thriving reality with 'Sales and Scale.' Your adventure in mastering the art and science of marketing and sales starts now.

Be A Unicorn: The New Entrepreneur's Ultimate Guide To Success

Dream It, Build It:
An Aspirational Odyssey Through
Entrepreneurship in Ten Inspiring Volumes.

Volume Six

SALES AND SCALE
The Entrepreneur's Blueprint for Mastering Marketing
and Achieving Explosive Growth

1

Understanding Your Target Market

"The aim of marketing is to know and understand the customer so well the product or service fits him and sells itself."
— Peter Drucker

Navigating the intricate world of marketing and sales, the cornerstone of any triumphant strategy lies in a profound understanding of your target market. the key to unlocking true business potential lies not just in the products or services offered but in a nuanced understanding of those they are intended for. This chapter serves as a guide through the art and science of identifying and understanding your target market, a critical step in tailoring your strategies to meet the specific needs and desires of your audience. It delves into the techniques for conducting comprehensive market research, segmenting your audience, and creating detailed customer profiles, all aimed at ensuring your marketing efforts hit the mark with precision and effectiveness.

A deep dive into market analysis reveals not just the who, but the why behind consumer choices, enabling businesses to craft solutions that are not merely seen but felt by their intended audience. This chapter explores how to gather and interpret market data, segment audiences for targeted marketing, and develop buyer personas that bring your target market to life. Through this process, entrepreneurs can transform abstract market concepts into tangible strategies that resonate on a personal level with potential customers.

As we unpack the layers of market understanding, we underscore the importance of empathy in marketing. It's about seeing the world through your customers' eyes, understanding their pains, and rejoicing in their joys. This empathetic approach not only sharpens your marketing messages but also aligns product development with genuine customer needs, creating a seamless bridge between what you offer and what your audience seeks.

Opening Anecdote: The Spanx Revolution: Shaping an Industry with Insight

In the late 1990s, Sara Blakely, armed with nothing but grit, a revolutionary idea, and $5,000, embarked on a journey that would redefine women's undergarments. Frustrated by the lack of suitable options that seamlessly blended comfort with control, Blakely envisioned Spanx, a brand that would introduce body-shaping undergarments designed to solve wardrobe woes for women everywhere. Her deep understanding of the target market's needs, combined with an unwavering commitment to innovation, catapulted Spanx from a one-woman operation to a global powerhouse, revolutionizing the industry and setting a new standard for product development driven by customer insight.

> *Quick Thought:*
> *Understanding transcends demographics; it's about empathizing with the core challenges and aspirations of your audience.*

Entrepreneurship in Action: Key Ingredients

- **Insightful Research:** Start with a foundation of robust market research. Dive deep into understanding the intricacies of your market, identifying not just who your customers are but, more importantly, why they seek solutions like yours.
- **Segmentation Strategy:** Break down your broad audience into manageable, targeted segments. This nuanced approach allows for more personalized and effective marketing strategies.
- **Persona Development:** Craft detailed buyer personas. These fictional yet data-driven profiles of your ideal customers guide tailored marketing efforts, ensuring messages resonate on a personal level.

Case Study: Dollar Shave Club's Market Disruption

Dollar Shave Club's entrance into the grooming industry was nothing short of revolutionary, offering a compelling solution to a common frustration: the inconvenience and expense of purchasing quality razors. With a keen insight into the grievances of their target demographic—men weary of overpriced razors—the brand positioned itself as a disruptor

3

from the outset.

- **The Vision:** To redefine the razor market by providing a convenient, cost-effective alternative to the traditional razor buying experience, directly addressing the consumer pain points of cost and accessibility.
- **The Challenge:** Breaking into a market dominated by longstanding, established brands with a new value proposition: high-quality, affordable razors delivered directly to customers' doors.
- **The Approach:** Dollar Shave Club's strategy hinged on direct and engaging marketing. Utilizing humor and clear, relatable messaging, they connected with their audience on a personal level, making their value proposition undeniable. The brand harnessed the power of social media and viral marketing to amplify their message, quickly rising above the industry noise.
- **The Impact:** The company's approach led to rapid growth, a fervently loyal customer base, and a seismic shift in the grooming industry, culminating in a $1 billion acquisition by Unilever. Dollar Shave Club's trajectory is a testament to the effectiveness of understanding and addressing customer needs with a mix of quality, value, and relatable branding.

Dollar Shave Club exemplifies how a clear understanding of the target market, combined with innovative marketing and a compelling value proposition, can disrupt established industries and redefine consumer expectations.

```
Pro Tip: Let your market research guide your
innovation. The more you know about your customers,
the better you can serve them with products and
services that feel tailor-made.
```

Exercise : Target Market Mastery

Conducting Market Research:

1. Identify key industry trends that impact your target market.
2. Design and execute a survey to uncover customer needs and preferences.
3. Analyze your competitors to find gaps in the market you can exploit.

Analyzing Customer Needs and Preferences:

1. Create a list of pain points your target market experiences.
2. Host a focus group to dive deeper into these pain points and potential solutions.
3. Map out the customer journey for your product or service, highlighting touchpoints where you can exceed expectations.

Creating Buyer Personas and Customer Segmentation:

1. Develop three to five buyer personas representing your core market segments.

2. For each persona, outline their demographic, psychographic, and behavioral traits.
3. Craft personalized messaging strategies for each persona, focusing on how your product or service solves their unique challenges.

Challenge For You: Pick a product or service you use regularly. Imagine you're tasked with marketing it to a new demographic. How would you adapt your strategies to resonate with this new audience? What research methods would you employ to ensure your approach is effective?

Conclusion:

Understanding your target market is not just about gathering data; it's about translating that knowledge into actionable insights that drive your marketing and sales strategies. By immersing yourself in the needs, preferences, and behaviors of your audience, you can craft offerings that genuinely resonate, fostering a connection that transcends the transactional. As we progress to exploring the intricacies of building a strong brand in the next chapter, remember that the foundation of all successful marketing endeavors is a deep, empathetic understanding of those you aim to serve.

2

Building a Strong Brand

"People will forget what you said, forget what you did, but people will never forget how you made them feel."
— Maya Angelou

Amidst an ever-evolving marketplace, building a brand that not only captures attention but also fosters a deep, enduring connection with consumers has become a critical endeavor for businesses aiming for longevity and success. This chapter explores the transformative journey of crafting such a brand, highlighting the significance of authenticity, alignment, and distinctiveness in resonating with today's discerning audiences. It examines the strategic process of defining what your brand stands for, how it communicates, and the experience it promises, ensuring that every facet of your brand harmoniously contributes to a compelling narrative that engages and inspires.

The path to brand strength is paved with clarity of purpose, consistency in message, and creativity in execution. This chapter delves into the foundational steps of identifying your brand's core mission and values, aligning them with the expectations and aspirations of your target audience, and articulating a unique brand personality that stands out in a crowded marketplace. Through a blend of strategic thinking and creative storytelling, businesses can forge a brand identity that not only distinguishes them from competitors but also deeply resonates with customers, turning fleeting interactions into lasting relationships.

Furthermore, this chapter underscores the dynamic nature of branding in the digital age, where brands are expected to not just speak but also listen and adapt. It presents a framework for ongoing brand evaluation and evolution, ensuring that your brand remains relevant and responsive to the changing landscapes of culture, technology, and consumer behavior. Through real-world examples and practical insights, we explore how successful brands navigate these challenges, continuously refining and redefining their identity to maintain a strong, meaningful presence in the lives of their consumers.

Opening Anecdote: The Rebirth of Old Spice: From Dated to Iconic

Once perceived as a brand for the previous generation, Old Spice reimagined its image through a groundbreaking campaign that redefined its place in the market. With the launch of "The Man Your Man Could Smell Like" campaign, Old Spice injected vitality and humor into its brand, dramatically shifting public perception. This strategic pivot not only captivated a younger demographic but also revitalized the brand's identity, showcasing the transformative power of a strong, well-positioned brand.

Quick Thought:
  A brand's essence is its heartbeat; keep it consistent, yet adaptable to the rhythms of market changes and customer expectations.

Entrepreneurship in Action: Key Ingredients

- **Authentic Purpose:** Begin with a clear, authentic purpose. Your brand should reflect a mission that goes beyond profit, resonating with your audience on an emotional level.
- **Aligned Values:** Ensure your brand values mirror those of your target audience. This alignment fosters a deeper connection and loyalty among your customer base.
- **Distinct Personality:** Your brand's personality should be distinctive and consistent across all interactions, making your business memorable and relatable.

Case Study: The LEGO Group's Brand Evolution

The LEGO Group's remarkable turnaround from the brink of bankruptcy in the early 2000s to becoming the world's leading toy company is a testament to the power of strategic brand reinvention focused on core values. By recentering on creativity, imagination, and the intrinsic joy of learning, LEGO set the foundation for a brand resurgence that would captivate millions around the globe.

- **The Vision:** To reinvigorate the LEGO brand by emphasizing its foundational pillars of creativity and quality, making

LEGO not just a toy but a tool for imagination across all ages.

- **The Challenge:** Overcoming financial turmoil and a diluted brand identity, LEGO needed to rediscover its essence and reinforce its value to consumers in a rapidly changing toy market.
- **The Approach:** LEGO embarked on a journey of brand revitalization, concentrating on high-quality, innovative products that sparked imagination. Themed sets and strategic collaborations catered to a broad audience, while ventures into movies and digital games expanded LEGO's narrative reach, enhancing brand engagement and connection.
- **The Impact:** LEGO's strategic renaissance not only averted financial collapse but also catapulted the company to unprecedented heights, securing its position as the preeminent toy manufacturer globally. Through a commitment to its core values and a knack for storytelling, LEGO has nurtured a dedicated and multi-generational fan base, demonstrating the enduring appeal of creativity and play.

LEGO's story of revival and growth underscores the significance of staying true to one's brand essence while innovating and adapting to the changing landscape, ensuring that the brand remains relevant and beloved by fans old and new.

Pro Tip: Consistency is key in branding, but so is evolution. Always be willing to refine and adapt your

brand to meet the changing needs and desires of your
audience without losing sight of your core values and
identity.

Exercise: Brand Building Workshop

Defining Your Brand Identity:

1. Write down the core purpose of your brand. Why does it exist beyond making a profit? Reflect on how it improves the lives of your customers or the world at large.
2. List the top five values your brand embodies. Consider how these values align with those of your target audience and how they're reflected in your operations and offerings.
3. Describe your brand's personality in three adjectives. Consider how these traits should be communicated through your brand's tone, style, and customer interactions.

Crafting Compelling Brand Messaging:

1. Develop your brand's story, focusing on its origins, challenges, triumphs, and mission. How does your story connect emotionally with your audience?
2. Define your unique value proposition (UVP). What makes your brand stand out from the competition? Ensure it's clear, compelling, and concise.
3. Create a messaging framework that includes key messages, taglines, and calls to action. Ensure they are consistent across all platforms and resonate with your target audi-

ence.

Creating a Consistent Brand Experience:

1. Design or refine your logo, color scheme, and typography. Ensure these visual elements are cohesive and reflect your brand's personality and values.
2. Draft brand guidelines that cover visual and verbal communication. This document should guide anyone who creates content for your brand, ensuring consistency.
3. Identify all customer touchpoints with your brand, from social media to customer service. Evaluate whether each touchpoint consistently reflects your brand identity and experience.

Challenge For You: Conduct a "brand audit" of your current business or a brand you admire. Assess the consistency of its identity, messaging, and experience across different platforms and touchpoints. Identify areas for improvement and propose changes that could strengthen the brand's coherence and impact.

Conclusion:

The journey of building a strong brand is both an art and a science. It requires a deep understanding of your brand's core identity, a clear articulation of its value, and the diligent application of these elements across all aspects of your business. Through the lens of impactful brands like Old Spice and LEGO, we've seen how authenticity, innovation, and consistency can elevate a brand from mere relevance to iconic status.

As you move forward, remember that your brand is a living

entity that should evolve with your audience and the market. By staying true to your brand's purpose, values, and personality while adapting to new opportunities and challenges, you create a brand that not only survives but thrives.

3

Crafting a Marketing Strategy

"Marketing is no longer about the stuff that you make,
but about the stories you tell."
— Seth Godin

At the heart of every thriving business lies a meticulously crafted marketing strategy, a beacon that guides the way to reaching and engaging your target audience, elevating your brand, and achieving your overarching business goals. This chapter aims to illuminate the path toward developing such a strategy, one that harmonizes with the unique rhythms of your market, fostering a connection that goes beyond mere transactions to cultivate genuine brand loyalty. It provides a comprehensive framework for identifying your audience, selecting the most effective channels for engagement, and setting goals that align with your business aspirations, all while weaving the rich tapestry of your brand's story into the fabric of your marketing efforts.

At the crux of any successful marketing strategy is the profound understanding of whom you're speaking to—their desires, challenges, and the solutions they seek. This chapter delves into the techniques for gathering these insights, from data analytics to direct customer interactions, ensuring that every aspect of your marketing is informed by a deep empathy for your audience. It further explores how to leverage these insights to make strategic decisions about where to tell your brand's story, be it through social media, content marketing, or traditional advertising avenues, ensuring that your message is not just heard, but felt.

Moreover, this chapter emphasizes the significance of setting clear, actionable goals for your marketing endeavors and outlines methods for measuring success against these objectives. Through real-world examples and actionable advice, it demonstrates how a well-orchestrated marketing strategy can transform the way your audience perceives and interacts with your brand, turning casual observers into loyal customers and, ultimately, brand ambassadors.

Opening Anecdote: The Spotify Playlist Phenomenon: Tuning into User Preferences

Spotify's ascent in the digital music realm is a testament to the power of a customer-centric marketing strategy. By leveraging data analytics to understand user preferences, Spotify created personalized playlists, fostering an unparalleled listening experience. This approach not only heightened user engagement but also solidified Spotify's reputation as a brand that truly understands and values its audience's unique tastes.

Quick Thought:

Understanding your audience is the cornerstone of marketing; it turns generic interactions into meaningful connections.

Entrepreneurship in Action: Key Ingredients

- **In-depth Audience Insights:** Delve deep into your audience's world. Use market research, analytics, and direct feedback to grasp their needs, preferences, and behaviors.
- **Strategic Channel Selection:** Not all channels are equal. Choose the ones where your audience is most active and engaged. Whether it's digital, traditional, or experiential marketing, go where your audience is.
- **Goal-Oriented Planning:** Set specific, measurable, achievable, relevant, and time-bound (SMART) goals to steer your marketing efforts and gauge success.

Case Study: Glossier's Community-Driven Growth Strategy

Glossier, a beauty brand that emerged from a beauty blog, Into The Gloss, revolutionized the cosmetics industry by building its marketing strategy around user-generated content, community engagement, and digital-first experiences. Founded by Emily Weiss, Glossier leveraged its deep understanding of its target market to create products and a brand that resonated with millennials and Gen Z consumers who craved authenticity and inclusivity.

Approach: Glossier's strategy centered on leveraging social media to create a dialogue with its audience, turning customers into brand advocates. By encouraging the sharing of real-life beauty routines, Glossier cultivated a loyal community. They utilized feedback and insights from their community to inform product development, ensuring that their offerings directly reflected consumer desires and needs.

Impact: This community-driven approach led to explosive growth for Glossier. The brand successfully fostered a strong sense of belonging among its customer base, leading to high levels of customer loyalty and repeat purchases. Glossier's emphasis on community and inclusivity not only differentiated it from traditional beauty brands but also established it as a trailblazer in leveraging digital platforms for brand building and direct-to-consumer sales.

Glossier's success story underscores the potency of a marketing strategy that prioritizes customer engagement and community building. For entrepreneurs, it highlights the importance of listening to and involving your audience in your brand journey, demonstrating that when customers feel valued and heard, they become your most powerful marketing tool.

Pro Tip: Embrace the power of storytelling. A compelling narrative that resonates with your audience can transform your brand from a mere option to their preferred choice.

Exercise: Marketing Strategy Workshop

Audience Analysis:

1. Conduct a survey to understand the needs, preferences, and pain points of your target audience.
2. Analyze the data to identify trends and insights that can inform your marketing strategies.
3. Create detailed buyer personas to guide personalized marketing efforts.

Channel Strategy:

1. Evaluate the effectiveness of various marketing channels for your audience, including digital, traditional, and experiential.
2. Plan a multi-channel marketing campaign that leverages the strengths of each selected channel.
3. Monitor and adjust your channel strategy based on performance data and feedback.

Goal Setting and Measurement:

1. Define SMART goals for your marketing campaigns that align with your business objectives.
2. Identify key performance indicators (KPIs) to measure the success of your marketing efforts.
3. Regularly review your campaigns' performance, using analytics tools and customer feedback to optimize and refine your strategies.

Challenge For You: Identify a marketing campaign that impressed you, and dissect its components to understand what made it effective. How can you apply these insights to your own marketing strategy?

Conclusion:

A well-crafted marketing strategy transcends mere promotion, transforming into a narrative that connects with your audience on a personal level, addresses their needs, and aligns with their values. Through the lens of successful campaigns like Spotify's personalized playlists and Dollar Shave Club's viral launch, we see the potency of a strategy rooted in deep audience understanding, strategic channel selection, and clear goal orientation.

As you venture forward, let your marketing strategy be both a mirror reflecting your audience's aspirations and a window to the unique value your brand offers. Remember, the ultimate goal is to not just reach your audience but to resonate with them, fostering lasting connections that drive growth and brand loyalty.

4

Digital Marketing Strategies

"In the world of Internet Customer Service, it's important to remember your competitor is only one mouse click away."
— Doug Warner

Navigating the digital realm requires a savvy understanding of the vast array of tools and tactics at your disposal. Digital marketing stands as the vanguard for any entrepreneurial venture aiming to make a mark in the online world. This chapter aims to equip you with a comprehensive arsenal of digital marketing tactics, designed to amplify your online presence, engage meaningfully with your target audience, and drive measurable results. From the intricacies of SEO to the dynamic world of social media and beyond, we explore the pillars that uphold a successful digital marketing strategy, ensuring you're not just participating in the digital space but thriving within it.

As we delve into the nuances of each strategy, we emphasize the importance of a cohesive digital marketing plan—one that integrates various channels and tactics for a synergistic effect.

This holistic approach is crucial for cutting through the noise of the digital landscape, ensuring your message not only reaches its intended audience but also resonates and inspires action. Through practical insights, expert advice, and actionable steps, this chapter serves as your guide through the complex, ever-changing world of digital marketing.

Opening Anecdote: The Rise of Canva: Democratizing Design Through SEO and Content Marketing

Canva's meteoric rise in the digital design space highlights the power of leveraging digital marketing strategies effectively. By focusing on SEO and producing a wealth of valuable content aimed at solving user design challenges, Canva has not only enhanced its online visibility but also established itself as a go-to resource for millions seeking user-friendly design tools. This strategic approach has transformed Canva from a startup into a global powerhouse in digital design.

> ### Quick Thought:
> *Digital marketing is not just about broadcasting your message in the digital world; it's about strategically placing that message so it's seen by the right people at the right time.*

Entrepreneurship in Action: Key Ingredients

- **Strategic SEO Application:** Master the art of SEO to ensure your website and content rise to the top of search engine results, capturing valuable organic traffic.

- **PPC Campaign Precision:** Utilize pay-per-click advertising to target specific demographics with precision, ensuring your marketing budget is spent on leads most likely to convert.
- **Social Media Savvy:** Engage your audience where they spend their time online, using targeted content to foster community, loyalty, and brand advocacy.
- **Content Marketing Mastery:** Provide genuine value through content that educates, entertains, and informs, establishing your brand as a thought leader in your industry.

Case Study: The Buffer Blog's Impact on Social Media Marketing

Buffer has masterfully leveraged content marketing through its blog to emerge as a vanguard in social media strategy. Offering a wealth of knowledge from in-depth articles and cutting-edge research to practical insights into the latest social media trends, Buffer has crafted an indispensable resource for marketers and businesses alike.

- **The Vision:** To empower social media marketers with the knowledge and tools to excel in their campaigns, establishing Buffer as the go-to source for social media wisdom.
- **The Challenge:** Standing out in the crowded content marketing landscape, where every brand vies to establish thought leadership in social media marketing.
- **The Approach:** Buffer's strategy hinges on delivering

unparalleled value through its content, blending original research with actionable advice. This dedication to quality not only bolsters Buffer's SEO rankings but also nurtures a dedicated community of readers and users who rely on Buffer for their social media strategy needs.

- **The Impact:** The Buffer blog has significantly propelled the brand's website traffic and user engagement, translating into increased product adoption. This case study exemplifies the transformative power of content marketing in attracting, educating, and converting an audience, underscoring the efficacy of a well-executed content strategy in driving business growth.

Buffer's journey underscores the critical role of high-quality, informative content in establishing brand authority and fostering a loyal customer base in the digital marketing realm.

```
Pro Tip: Integrate your digital marketing efforts.
Ensure that SEO, PPC, social media, and content
marketing strategies support one another for a
cohesive and unified digital presence.
```

Exercise: Digital Marketing Strategy Workshop

SEO Strategy Development:

1. Perform comprehensive keyword research relevant to your niche and audience.
2. Audit your website to ensure it's optimized for speed,

mobile usage, and user experience.

3. Plan a content calendar that addresses your audience's questions and positions you as a solution provider.

PPC Campaign Planning:

1. Define clear objectives for your PPC campaigns, including target demographics and desired actions.
2. Craft compelling ad copy and visuals that resonate with your target audience.
3. Set up conversion tracking to measure the effectiveness of your campaigns and optimize accordingly.

Social Media Engagement Plan:

1. Choose platforms that align with your brand and where your target audience is most active.
2. Create a content plan that balances promotional, educational, and engaging content.
3. Schedule regular engagement activities, such as live sessions or Q&As, to foster community.

Content Marketing Initiative:

1. Identify key topics that will interest your audience and establish your brand's authority.
2. Develop a variety of content types (blogs, videos, infographics) to cater to different preferences.
3. Utilize analytics to measure engagement and refine your content strategy over time.

Challenge For You: Analyze a successful digital marketing campaign in your industry. Identify the strategies used and consider how similar tactics could be adapted for your own business. What lessons can you learn from their success?

Conclusion:

Digital marketing is an ever-evolving field that demands creativity, agility, and a strategic mindset. By embracing SEO, PPC, social media marketing, and content marketing, businesses can not only increase their online presence but also build meaningful relationships with their audience, driving growth and success in the digital age.

5

Content Marketing and Thought Leadership

"Content is king, but engagement is queen,
and the lady rules the house!"
— Mari Smith

I n an era where information is abundant but attention is scarce, content marketing and thought leadership emerge as critical pillars for building a memorable and authoritative brand presence. Through strategic content creation and dissemination, businesses have the unique opportunity to engage with their audience on a deeper level, establishing trust and loyalty that transcend transactional relationships. This chapter explores how entrepreneurs can leverage content marketing and thought leadership to not only inform and inspire their audience but also to weave a narrative that positions their brand as an indispensable resource in their respective industries.

The journey of content marketing is more than just producing and sharing content; it's about crafting messages that resonate, provoke thought, and spark conversation. Thought leadership, on the other hand, positions you and your brand as the go-to experts in your field, influencing opinions, trends, and ultimately, decision-making processes within your industry. Together, they form a synergistic approach that can significantly amplify your brand's voice and impact. Through practical insights and actionable strategies, this chapter aims to guide you through creating a content ecosystem that not only attracts but captivates and retains your audience.

Opening Anecdote: The TED Conferences: Enlightening Minds Through Content

TED's ascent from a conference to a global knowledge-sharing platform epitomizes the transformative power of content marketing. By offering free access to talks that educate, inspire, and provoke thoughts, TED has positioned itself as a beacon of thought leadership, reaching millions worldwide. This strategic move not only amplified its audience but also cemented TED's reputation as a hub for groundbreaking ideas and visionary thinkers.

> ### Quick Thought:
> *Effective content marketing doesn't interrupt the audience's experience; it enriches it, turning each interaction into an opportunity for growth and connection.*

Entrepreneurship in Action: Key Ingredients

- **Audience-Centric Content:** Tailor your content to meet

the specific needs and interests of your audience. It's about striking a chord with their aspirations, challenges, and curiosities.

- **Diverse Content Portfolio:** Utilize a variety of formats — from insightful blog posts and engaging videos to informative podcasts and compelling infographics — to cater to different preferences and touchpoints.
- **Consistent Value Delivery:** Ensure your content consistently offers value, whether by solving problems, providing insights, or inspiring action. It's the consistency that builds trust and loyalty over time.

Case Study: The Influence of Moz's Whiteboard Fridays

Moz's "Whiteboard Friday" series stands as a beacon of innovation in digital marketing education, transforming the way SEO knowledge is shared and consumed. By demystifying the often complex and ever-evolving landscape of SEO, Moz has made high-level strategies accessible to a wide audience, ranging from novices to seasoned professionals.

- **The Vision:** To empower individuals and businesses with the knowledge to navigate the complexities of SEO, thereby enhancing their online presence and effectiveness.
- **The Challenge:** Breaking down intricate SEO concepts into understandable, actionable advice without diluting the sophistication or value of the information.
- **The Approach:** Moz leverages the "Whiteboard Friday" series as a platform to distill complex SEO topics into clear, engaging, and actionable insights. This approach not only

educates but also builds a community of learners who are equipped to apply these insights to their digital marketing efforts.

- **The Impact:** The "Whiteboard Friday" initiative has significantly bolstered Moz's standing as an authoritative voice in SEO, driving substantial increases in website traffic and user engagement. This success highlights the importance of consistent, high-quality content in establishing thought leadership and fostering a loyal community of followers.

Pro Tip: Leverage every piece of content as a brick in building your brand's reputation. Each blog post, video, or social media update contributes to the bigger picture of your brand identity and authority.

Exercise: Crafting Your Content Marketing Blueprint

Audience Insight Gathering:

1. Dive deep into understanding your audience through surveys, social listening, and market research. Pinpoint their needs, challenges, and content consumption habits.
2. Develop comprehensive buyer personas to guide your content creation efforts.

Content Diversification Plan:

1. Map out a content strategy that includes a mix of formats

tailored to your audience's preferences and your brand's strengths. Experiment with different mediums to find what resonates best.

2. Schedule a consistent pipeline of content across chosen platforms, ensuring a steady stream of value to your audience.

Engagement and Measurement Framework:

1. Set clear objectives for each content piece, whether it's to educate, convert, or engage. Define KPIs that align with these objectives to measure success.
2. Regularly review analytics to gauge content performance, audience engagement, and areas for optimization. Adjust your strategy based on these insights to continuously improve and refine your approach.

Challenge For You: Identify a topic within your industry that has not been extensively covered or offers room for a new perspective. Create a comprehensive content piece on this topic, aiming to provide unique insights or solutions. Promote this content across your channels and measure its impact on your audience engagement and brand perception.

Conclusion:

Content marketing and thought leadership are integral to establishing a brand that not only speaks but is heard and valued in the crowded digital marketplace. By prioritizing value-rich content tailored to your audience's needs and positioning yourself as a reliable source of knowledge, you pave the way for deeper connections, enhanced brand loyalty, and sustained entrepreneurial growth.

As we progress, remember that the journey of content marketing is continuous, requiring adaptability, creativity, and a keen ear to the evolving needs of your audience. In the next chapter, we delve into the dynamics of effective customer acquisition strategies, exploring how to convert your engaged audience into loyal customers and brand advocates.

6

Effective Customer Acquisition

"Customers are like teeth. Ignore them and they'll go away."
— Jerry Flanagan

This chapter dives deep into the multifaceted world of customer acquisition, exploring innovative strategies that can attract, engage, and convert prospects into loyal customers. From leveraging digital platforms to mastering the nuances of consumer psychology, the journey towards building a thriving customer base is both complex and rewarding.

The essence of successful customer acquisition lies in understanding and implementing a blend of tactics that resonate with your target audience while differentiating your brand in a crowded market. It's about creating value that speaks directly to potential customers, making your offering irresistible. This chapter will guide you through identifying the most effective channels for your business, crafting compelling messaging that captivates prospects, and employing tactical marketing strategies that drive conversion. Through a comprehensive exploration of customer acquisition techniques, you'll learn how to systematically grow your customer base and scale your business effectively.

Central to this exploration is the concept that every interaction with a potential customer is an opportunity to tell your brand's story, to demonstrate your value, and to build a relationship that transcends the initial sale. The strategies discussed in this chapter are designed to not only capture attention but to foster trust and loyalty, ensuring that each new customer becomes a lasting advocate for your brand.

Opening Anecdote: Tesla's Disruption Through Customer Experience

Tesla's approach to customer acquisition, focusing on exceptional product quality and a revolutionary buying experience, underscores the impact of customer-centric strategies in today's market. By sidestepping traditional dealership models and engaging customers directly through sleek showrooms and online platforms, Tesla has not only sold cars but also its vision of the future, capturing the imagination and loyalty of a global audience.

Quick Thought:

At its core, acquiring customers is about forming connections. It's a dance of discovery where businesses and consumers find common ground, fueled by shared values and needs.

Entrepreneurship in Action: Key Ingredients

- **Target Audience Clarity:** A deep dive into who your customers are, their needs, preferences, and pain points, is foundational. The sharper your audience insight, the more targeted and effective your acquisition efforts can be.
- **Strategic Content Creation:** Content that educates, entertains, and solves problems attracts potential customers. It's about adding value to their lives before asking for anything in return.
- **Seamless Conversion Pathways:** The journey from interest to purchase should be as frictionless as possible. Optimize every touchpoint to guide potential customers smoothly towards making a buying decision.

Case Study: Shopify's Empowerment of Entrepreneurs

Shopify has redefined the e-commerce landscape by championing a model of empowerment for small businesses and entrepreneurs. Recognizing the burgeoning potential of digital retail, Shopify has positioned itself as an indispensable ally to those looking to forge their path in the online marketplace.

- **The Vision:** To democratize e-commerce by providing intuitive, accessible tools that enable anyone, regardless of technical skill, to launch and grow an online store.
- **The Challenge:** In a digital age where the e-commerce space is increasingly crowded and complex, the challenge was to stand out as more than just a platform, but as a catalyst for entrepreneurial success.
- **The Approach:** Shopify's strategy has been multifaceted, focusing on educating its users with comprehensive guides,

34

offering robust support systems, and fostering a vibrant community of like-minded entrepreneurs. This holistic support system positions Shopify not merely as a service provider but as a partner vested in the success of its users.

- **The Impact:** The commitment to empowering entrepreneurs has not only fostered a deeply loyal user base but has also propelled Shopify to the forefront of e-commerce solutions. Shopify's journey from a nascent startup to a leading platform underscores the power of user empowerment in driving business success and loyalty.

Shopify's success story serves as a blueprint for how platforms can thrive by genuinely empowering their users. By equipping entrepreneurs with the tools, knowledge, and support to succeed, Shopify has cultivated a thriving ecosystem of digital retail, showcasing the transformative power of empowerment in the e-commerce domain.

Pro Tip: Keep the focus on solving problems. When your product or service resolves a significant pain point, it naturally attracts those in need of solutions, making acquisition a byproduct of your value proposition.

Exercise: Crafting Your Customer Acquisition Framework

Audience Definition and Research:

1. Embark on a detailed analysis of your target market. Utilize tools and techniques like surveys, interviews, and social media analytics to gather insights.
2. Develop precise buyer personas to guide your marketing strategies and content creation.

Multi-Channel Marketing Strategy:

1. Identify and prioritize marketing channels based on where your target audience spends their time. Consider a mix of digital and traditional channels tailored to your audience's habits.
2. Craft channel-specific strategies to engage your audience effectively, from SEO and content marketing to social media and email campaigns.

Conversion Optimization Tactics:

1. Analyze your current conversion funnel for bottlenecks and areas for improvement. Implement changes aimed at simplifying the buying process.
2. Regularly test and tweak your website and landing pages to enhance usability, message clarity, and call-to-action visibility.

Challenge For You: Select a product or service in your

portfolio that has been challenging to sell. Re-evaluate your approach to acquiring customers for this offering, applying the insights and strategies discussed in this chapter. Implement a revised customer acquisition plan and monitor the results closely.

Conclusion:

Effective customer acquisition is both an art and a science, requiring a blend of strategic insight, creative engagement, and relentless optimization. By understanding your audience deeply, leveraging multiple channels to reach them, and ensuring a seamless conversion experience, you set the stage for not just transactions, but lasting relationships.

As we continue our exploration, remember that acquisition is just the beginning. In the following chapters, we'll delve into the nuances of nurturing these relationships, fostering loyalty, and encouraging advocacy, which are essential for long-term success in the entrepreneurial landscape.

7

Sales Techniques and Strategies

"People don't like to be sold, but they love to buy."
— Jeffrey Gitomer

The intricate dance of sales, an art steeped in persuasion and influence, demands not just understanding what your potential customers want but aligning your offerings so compellingly that the decision to buy becomes natural. This chapter embarks on a journey to explore the art and science behind effective sales techniques and strategies, essential tools for entrepreneurs looking to thrive in the competitive marketplace. By weaving together a tapestry of best practices, innovative approaches, and timeless principles, we aim to equip you with the means to not only reach but resonate with your audience, transforming prospects into devoted customers.

The essence of sales lies in understanding the delicate balance between offering solutions and fostering genuine connections. It's about transcending the transactional nature of business to create experiences that are meaningful, memorable, and motivational. From uncovering the nuanced desires of your target market to articulating the distinctive value of your offerings, this chapter delves into strategies that are designed to position your products or services as indispensable to your customers' lives or businesses. We explore how to navigate the complexities of the sales process, employing tactics that are both ethical and effective, ensuring that your venture not only survives but thrives in today's fast-paced business landscape.

Moreover, this exploration acknowledges the evolving nature of sales in the digital age, where the lines between marketing and sales blur, giving rise to integrated strategies that leverage content, technology, and personalization to attract, engage, and delight customers. Through a blend of traditional wisdom and modern methodologies, we uncover how to harness the full spectrum of sales techniques—from the persuasive power of storytelling to the precision of data-driven selling—to achieve sustained business growth.

Opening Anecdote: Zappos' Revolutionary Approach to Customer Service

Zappos, the online shoe and clothing retailer, transformed the landscape of online shopping with a radical focus on customer service as a sales strategy. By offering free returns, a 365-day return policy, and above all, a customer service team empowered to go the extra mile, Zappos not only sold shoes; they delivered happiness, creating a legion of loyal customers and setting a new benchmark in e-commerce.

> **Quick Thought:**
> *Sales is not about convincing customers to make a purchase; it's about creating an environment where the decision to buy becomes an obvious choice.*

Entrepreneurship in Action: Key Ingredients

- **Deep Market Understanding:** Know your audience inside out—what drives them, their challenges, and what solutions they are seeking.
- **Value-Based Selling:** Focus on the value your product or service brings to the customer, tailoring your pitch to highlight how it solves their specific problems.
- **Relationship Over Transactions:** Prioritize building long-term relationships with your customers over making a quick sale. Trust and loyalty are the cornerstones of repeated business and referrals.

Case Study: HubSpot's Inbound Sales Philosophy

HubSpot, at the forefront of inbound marketing and sales, has fundamentally shifted the business sales paradigm. By championing an approach that prioritizes attracting, engaging, and delighting customers, HubSpot has introduced a more human and helpful way to grow businesses, moving away from traditional interruptive sales tactics.

- **The Vision:** To transform the sales process into a value-driven journey, where businesses attract customers by being genuinely helpful and providing solutions that address their needs.

- **The Challenge:** In a landscape saturated with aggressive sales tactics, the challenge was to prove that a more consultative, inbound approach could lead to better long-term customer relationships and business growth.
- **The Approach:** HubSpot's strategy revolves around creating and distributing valuable content and tools that speak directly to the challenges and pain points of their target audience. This content-first approach ensures that potential customers are naturally drawn to HubSpot, facilitating a sales process that is more about solving problems than pushing products.
- **The Impact:** Embracing this inbound sales philosophy has not only reinforced HubSpot's position as a leader in the digital marketing and sales space but also contributed to its rapid growth. By aligning sales strategies with customer needs and the principles of inbound marketing, HubSpot demonstrates the efficacy of building trust and providing value ahead of the sale.

HubSpot's success story is a testament to the power and potential of the inbound methodology, showcasing how aligning with customer needs and focusing on providing value can revolutionize sales strategies and drive significant business growth.

Pro Tip: Always be listening. The more you listen to your customers, the more you understand their needs, which enables you to offer solutions that feel personalized and, therefore, more compelling.

Exercise: Refining Your Sales Strategy

Market and Audience Analysis:

1. Conduct thorough research on your target market and audience. Understand their buying behavior, preferences, and the channels they frequent.
2. Develop buyer personas to tailor your sales approach and messaging to meet the unique needs of different customer segments.

Value Proposition and Messaging:

1. Clearly articulate the value your product or service provides. Focus on the benefits and solutions it offers to your target audience's specific challenges.
2. Craft compelling sales messages that resonate with your audience, emphasizing how your offerings can make a positive difference in their lives or businesses.

Building and Nurturing Customer Relationships:

1. Implement strategies for ongoing engagement with your customers, such as regular follow-ups, personalized communications, and loyalty programs.
2. Encourage feedback and be responsive to your customers' needs and concerns, adapting your offerings and services to serve them better.

Challenge For You: Identify a segment of your target audience that has been challenging to convert. Utilize the insights and strategies from this chapter to develop a tailored approach for this segment, focusing on their specific needs and how your offerings can meet those needs. Monitor the results and refine your strategy based on the feedback and outcomes.

Conclusion:

Mastering sales is about more than just techniques and strategies; it's about creating genuine connections, understanding and solving for the customer's needs, and consistently delivering value. By adopting a customer-centric approach, focusing on building relationships, and leveraging the power of inbound sales, entrepreneurs can not only achieve their sales goals but also build a loyal customer base that fuels sustainable business growth.

8

Customer Relationship Management (CRM)

"The goal as a company is to have customer service that is not just the best but legendary."
— Sam Walton

In an era where customer expectations continually evolve and personalization becomes not just preferred but expected, mastering Customer Relationship Management (CRM) is essential for businesses aspiring to thrive. CRM extends beyond a mere database of customer interactions; it is a comprehensive approach to understanding, engaging, and delighting customers at every touchpoint of their journey with your brand. This chapter aims to unravel the strategic significance of CRM, showcasing how it can serve as the backbone of not only enhancing customer loyalty but also optimizing operational efficiency and driving informed, data-driven growth strategies.

Through the lens of CRM, businesses gain the capability to transform vast amounts of customer data into actionable insights, enabling personalized marketing, sales, and service strategies that significantly enhance the customer experience. By integrating CRM practices, entrepreneurs can ensure that every customer interaction is informed and meaningful, thereby building deeper relationships that contribute to long-term business success. This chapter explores the foundational elements of effective CRM systems, including the integration of technology, processes, and people to create a unified approach to customer management. It highlights how CRM facilitates a more personalized and responsive engagement with customers, leading to increased satisfaction and loyalty.

Effective CRM also empowers businesses to streamline internal processes, ensuring that customer-facing teams have the information they need to provide exceptional service. It lays the groundwork for a culture that values and utilizes customer insights to drive decision-making, product development, and innovation. Through real-world examples and practical insights, this chapter provides a roadmap for entrepreneurs to leverage CRM as a strategic tool for building a customer-centric business model that not only attracts but retains customers, ensuring sustainable growth and a competitive edge in the market.

Opening Anecdote: Salesforce's Trailblazing CRM Journey

Salesforce revolutionized CRM by transitioning it to the cloud, making customer data accessible anytime, anywhere. This innovation not only democratized CRM for businesses of all sizes but also underscored the importance of real-time, actionable customer insights in crafting personalized experiences. Salesforce's approach exemplifies how technology can transform customer management from a reactive to a proactive and predictive strategy, setting new standards for customer engagement and satisfaction.

> *Quick Thought:*
> *CRM is not just a technology but a philosophy—a commitment to putting the customer at the heart of the business.*

Entrepreneurship in Action: Key Ingredients

- **Holistic Customer View:** A 360-degree view of the customer enables personalized interactions and offers insights into their preferences and behaviors, paving the way for enhanced customer experiences.
- **Streamlined Processes:** Efficient CRM systems automate routine tasks, freeing up time for teams to focus on strategic, customer-centric activities.
- **Data-Driven Decisions:** Leveraging customer data for insights guides more informed business decisions, from product development to marketing strategies.

Case Study: Sephora's Personalized Beauty Experience

Sephora has redefined the beauty retail landscape through its innovative use of Customer Relationship Management (CRM) to offer a personalized shopping journey that captivates customers both digitally and within its stores. Recognizing the diverse needs and preferences of its clientele, Sephora leveraged technology to transform how beauty enthusiasts discover and interact with products, creating a highly customized and engaging shopping experience.

- **The Vision:** To pioneer a beauty retail experience that feels personal, intuitive, and enriching for every customer, thereby setting a new standard for customer engagement in the beauty industry.
- **The Challenge:** Bridging the gap between the vast array of beauty products available and the unique beauty preferences of each customer, ensuring a personalized shopping experience that accurately reflects individual tastes and needs.
- **The Approach:** Central to Sephora's strategy is the Beauty Insider loyalty program, which gathers detailed customer data including purchase history, product preferences, and beauty interests. This rich dataset enables Sephora to curate personalized product recommendations, craft targeted promotions, and provide customized beauty advice, ensuring that each customer's experience is both personal and memorable.
- **The Impact:** Sephora's strategic use of CRM has fortified customer loyalty and propelled the brand to new heights

of business success. By leveraging data to refine marketing and sales tactics, Sephora has crafted a seamless omnichannel experience that resonates deeply with customers, encouraging repeated engagement and fostering a sense of community among beauty enthusiasts.

Sephora's commitment to personalization has not only enhanced the beauty shopping experience but also established the brand as a frontrunner in leveraging technology for customer satisfaction and business growth, showcasing the transformative power of CRM in creating lasting customer relationships and driving retail innovation.

```
Pro Tip: Regularly review and cleanse your CRM data.
Accurate, up-to-date information is crucial for
effective customer engagement and personalization.
```

Exercise: Implementing CRM in Your Business

CRM Selection and Implementation:

1. Assess your business needs and customer management challenges to select a CRM system that best fits your requirements.
2. Prioritize CRM features that support your specific sales, marketing, and customer service processes.

Customer Data Analysis:

1. Develop a plan for collecting, analyzing, and acting on customer data. Identify key customer metrics that will inform your business strategies.
2. Use data segmentation to tailor your marketing efforts and sales approaches to different customer groups.

CRM Training and Adoption:

1. Invest in comprehensive training for your team to ensure they are proficient in using the CRM system.
2. Foster a culture that values customer data and insights as essential tools for meeting customer needs and driving business success.

Challenge For You: Identify a segment of your customer base that has not been fully engaged or maximized. Utilize your CRM system to analyze their behavior and preferences, and design a targeted campaign to re-engage them, measuring the impact on customer loyalty and revenue.

Conclusion:

Effective CRM is transformative, enabling businesses to evolve from transactional entities to customer-centric organizations. By integrating CRM into your business strategy, you unlock the potential to not only meet but exceed customer expectations, ensuring your brand remains relevant and competitive in a rapidly changing market landscape.

As we move forward, our journey will take us into the realms of innovation and creativity, exploring their critical role in sustaining entrepreneurial ventures and driving them to new heights of success.

9

Influencer Marketing and Partnerships

**"People do not buy goods and services.
They buy relations, stories, and magic."
— Maya Angelou**

In today's hyper-connected world, the currency of successful marketing has shifted from mere visibility to authentic connection. Influencer marketing and strategic partnerships have emerged as powerful conduits to bridge the gap between brands and consumers, fostering trust and enhancing brand narratives through voices that audiences already know and respect. This chapter explores the strategic landscape of influencer marketing, detailing how entrepreneurs can effectively leverage influencers to amplify their brand's presence and authenticity. Through careful selection, creative collaboration, and focused execution, influencer partnerships can transform the way brands engage with their markets, turning casual observers into loyal advocates.

The rise of influencer marketing underscores a fundamental

shift in consumer behavior: people trust people, not ads. Influencers, with their cultivated communities and personal brand, offer a unique opportunity for businesses to humanize their interactions and weave their products into the fabric of daily life. This chapter will guide you through identifying the right influencers for your brand, crafting mutually beneficial partnerships, and creating content that resonates with and enriches your target audience's experience. By integrating influencers into your marketing mix, you can create more relatable, trustworthy, and engaging brand stories.

Yet, navigating the influencer marketing world requires more than just matching your brand with popular figures; it demands strategic planning, clear communication, and a focus on authenticity and values alignment. This chapter provides a blueprint for establishing successful influencer relationships, from understanding the nuances of influencer engagement to measuring the impact of your collaborations. Through real-world examples and actionable insights, you'll learn how to harness the power of influencer marketing to drive brand awareness, customer loyalty, and ultimately, business growth.

Opening Anecdote: The Daniel Wellington Phenomenon

Daniel Wellington's ascent to a global watch brand phenomenon highlights the transformative power of influencer marketing. By partnering with hundreds of influencers across different scales, the brand leveraged Instagram to showcase its minimalist timepieces, not through high-budget campaigns, but through genuine, lifestyle-oriented posts. This strategy not only skyrocketed their sales but also set a precedent for how emerging brands can achieve exponential growth through strategic influencer collaborations.

> **Quick Thought:**
> *The essence of influencer marketing lies in authenticity. It's about forging genuine connections between brands and their audiences through the voices of those they trust and admire.*

Entrepreneurship in Action: Key Ingredients

- **Alignment with Brand Values:** Choose influencers who resonate with your brand's ethos. Their authenticity becomes your authenticity in the eyes of potential customers.
- **Engagement Over Numbers:** Look beyond follower counts to engagement rates. Influencers who cultivate genuine interactions with their audience can offer more value.
- **Creativity and Collaboration:** Encourage creative freedom, allowing influencers to integrate your brand into their narrative in a way that feels natural to their audience.

Case Study: Gymshark's Community Building Mastery

Gymshark stands as a paradigm of how a brand can ascend to global prominence by intertwining influencer marketing with community building. In the crowded fitness apparel market, Gymshark distinguished itself not merely by selling products but by cultivating a sense of belonging among fitness enthusiasts. This strategy hinged on forging authentic connections with influencers and their audiences, who resonate with Gymshark's core values of motivation, inclusivity, and fitness as a lifestyle.

- **The Vision:** To transcend traditional marketing boundaries by creating a fitness community that is deeply connected to the Gymshark brand, fostering loyalty and enthusiasm.
- **The Challenge:** Differentiating itself in the highly competitive fitness apparel industry by not only promoting products but also nurturing a genuine community spirit among its target audience.
- **The Approach:** Gymshark adeptly leveraged long-term partnerships with fitness influencers, integrating these influencers into the fabric of their brand narrative. Through sponsorships and collaborations, Gymshark and its influencers produced content that was both authentic and inspirational, resonating deeply with the fitness community.
- **The Impact:** This innovative approach to influencer partnerships and community engagement has elevated Gymshark from a startup to a globally recognized brand, underscoring the transformative potential of influencer marketing when coupled with a genuine commitment to community building.

Gymshark's journey exemplifies the potency of community-centric marketing strategies in establishing a brand's identity and fueling its growth. By prioritizing authentic relationships and shared values, Gymshark has not only achieved remarkable business success but also inspired a global community of fitness enthusiasts.

```
Pro Tip: Transparency is key. Ensure clear
communication with both influencers and your audience
about the nature of your partnerships to maintain
trust and credibility.
```

Exercise: Crafting Your Influencer Marketing Strategy

Influencer Collaboration Blueprint

1. Create a matrix to evaluate potential influencers based on their alignment with your brand values and their ability to engage your target audience. Consider factors such as content style, audience demographics, and engagement rates. Rank influencers to prioritize outreach efforts.
2. Develop a detailed plan for reaching out to your top-ranked influencers, including personalized messaging that resonates with their personal brand and highlights mutual benefits. Include strategies for nurturing these relationships over time, turning initial contacts into lasting partnerships.
3. Draft a template for collaboration agreements that outlines expectations, deliverables, timelines, and compensation (if applicable). Ensure clarity and transparency to lay the foundation for a successful partnership.

Campaign Innovation and Management

1. Host a brainstorming session with your team or with potential influencer partners to generate innovative ideas for your next influencer campaign. Focus on concepts that align with both your brand's and the influencer's narrative, ensuring authenticity and engagement.
2. Create a comprehensive checklist covering all stages of campaign execution, from influencer briefing and content creation to launch and promotion. This checklist should ensure all aspects of the campaign are aligned with the agreed strategy and objectives.
3. Organize a workshop with your influencer partners to co-create content for the campaign. This collaborative approach encourages creativity and leverages the influencer's insight into what resonates best with their audience, enhancing campaign authenticity and effectiveness.

Evaluating Success and Impact

1. Design a dashboard to track key performance metrics of your influencer campaigns, such as reach, engagement, conversion rates, and ROI. This tool will help you monitor campaign success and gather insights for future strategies.
2. Schedule a debrief session with your influencer partners following a campaign to discuss performance, gather feedback, and identify areas for improvement. This reflective practice fosters learning and strengthens partnerships.
3. Compile an impact report summarizing the campaign's achievements, lessons learned, and areas for improvement. Use this report to inform future influencer marketing strategies, refining approaches based on empirical evidence and partner feedback.

Challenge For You

Using the exercises outlined above, launch a targeted influencer marketing campaign aimed at engaging a specific segment of your audience that has been challenging to reach. Implement the campaign, track its performance using your metrics dashboard, and conduct a comprehensive analysis to identify key takeaways and opportunities for optimization in future campaigns.

Conclusion:

Influencer marketing and strategic partnerships offer a dynamic and impactful way to reach and resonate with audiences in today's fragmented media landscape. By prioritizing authenticity, alignment, and creative collaboration, entrepreneurs can leverage these strategies to not only amplify their brand's reach but also to embed it within the narratives of their consumers' daily lives. As we move forward, embracing these modern marketing paradigms will be pivotal in crafting compelling brand stories and fostering lasting customer relationships.

Next, we will explore the intricate world of measuring marketing ROI, providing a framework to assess the effectiveness of your marketing initiatives and their contribution to your business's overall success.

10

Measuring Marketing ROI

"Not everything that can be counted counts,
and not everything that counts can be counted."
— William Bruce Cameron

I n an era where the digital footprint of businesses continues to expand exponentially, the ability to quantify the impact of marketing efforts through Return on Investment (ROI) analysis has become indispensable. It's no longer sufficient to launch campaigns based on intuition; today's entrepreneurs need to harness the power of data to drive their marketing decisions. This chapter is dedicated to unraveling the complexities of measuring marketing ROI, providing you with the methodologies to not only assess but also amplify the efficacy of your marketing endeavors. It's about transforming raw data into actionable insights that can steer your marketing strategy towards higher profitability and effectiveness.

The pursuit of a robust marketing ROI goes beyond mere number crunching; it involves a strategic synthesis of analytics, creativity, and market understanding. Here, you'll learn how to align your marketing objectives with measurable outcomes, select appropriate metrics that reflect your business goals, and leverage technology to track and analyze these metrics effectively. The aim is to create a feedback loop where every marketing action is scrutinized for its contribution to the bottom line, enabling you to optimize your strategies in real-time and allocate resources to the most productive channels.

Moreover, this chapter sheds light on the significance of viewing marketing ROI not just as a financial metric but as a comprehensive measure of customer engagement, brand equity, and market penetration. By incorporating both quantitative and qualitative analyses, you'll be equipped to make informed decisions that encompass the full spectrum of marketing's impact on your business. Through illustrative case studies and proven methodologies, we aim to guide you through the process of establishing a metrics-driven marketing culture that prioritizes results while fostering innovation and customer-centricity.

Opening Anecdote: The LEGO Group's Strategic Turnaround

The LEGO Group's remarkable comeback story is a testament to the power of strategic marketing investments and meticulous ROI analysis. Faced with financial struggles in the early 2000s, LEGO revamped its marketing approach, focusing on engaging directly with its core audience through innovative platforms and community-building efforts. By rigorously measuring the ROI of these initiatives, LEGO not only regained its footing but soared to new heights, becoming one of the most beloved and profitable toy manufacturers in the world.

> **Quick Thought:**
> *True mastery in marketing comes from understanding not just how to capture attention, but how to convert that attention into measurable results that drive business forward.*

Entrepreneurship in Action: Key Ingredients

- **Precision in Measurement:** Employ accurate tools and methodologies to track the ROI of marketing activities, ensuring data integrity for reliable analysis.
- **Strategic Adaptation:** Use ROI insights to nimbly adapt marketing strategies, focusing efforts on high-return activities to maximize effectiveness.
- **Holistic Viewpoint:** Consider both quantitative and qualitative metrics to gauge the comprehensive impact of marketing efforts on customer behavior and brand perception.

Case Study: Warby Parker's Direct-to-Consumer Success

Warby Parker emerged as a visionary force in the eyewear industry by pioneering a direct-to-consumer approach that fundamentally transformed how glasses are marketed and sold. With a keen focus on leveraging digital platforms to connect with customers, Warby Parker has not only democratized access to stylish, affordable eyewear but has also set new benchmarks for customer engagement in the digital age.

- **The Vision:** To revolutionize the eyewear purchasing experience through a customer-centric model that combines style, convenience, and affordability.
- **The Challenge:** Overcoming the traditional brick-and-mortar retail model in the eyewear industry, which often resulted in high prices and limited options for consumers.
- **The Approach:** Warby Parker implemented a robust digital marketing strategy, underpinned by rigorous analysis of key performance metrics such as conversion rates, customer acquisition costs, and customer lifetime value. Central to their strategy was an innovative try-before-you-buy service, allowing customers to select multiple frames to try at home for free, thereby enhancing the buying experience and fostering trust.
- **The Impact:** Through its meticulous, data-driven marketing strategies and unwavering commitment to customer satisfaction, Warby Parker has achieved rapid growth, cultivating a loyal customer base and redefining industry standards. This success story highlights the effectiveness of integrating ROI-focused marketing tactics with innovative customer service models to scale a business and disrupt traditional market dynamics.

Warby Parker's ascent is a compelling testament to the power of direct-to-consumer models in building brand loyalty and reshaping industries, illustrating how innovative approaches to customer engagement can create lasting success in the digital marketplace.

```
Pro Tip: Embrace experimentation. The path to
maximizing marketing ROI often involves testing new
approaches, learning from failures, and continuously
refining strategies based on data-driven insights.
```

Exercise: Enhancing Your Marketing ROI

Setting the Stage for Measurement

1. Identify specific marketing objectives for the upcoming quarter. For each objective, select 2-3 Key Performance Indicators (KPIs) that will help you measure the success of your efforts towards these goals. Ensure that these KPIs are SMART (Specific, Measurable, Achievable, Relevant, Time-bound).
2. Evaluate your current marketing tracking tools and systems. Identify any gaps in data collection and implement solutions to ensure comprehensive tracking across all marketing channels. This may involve integrating new analytics software, setting up conversion tracking pixels, or enhancing CRM data capture methods.
3. Conduct a thorough analysis of your current marketing performance, establishing benchmarks for your chosen KPIs. This historical data will serve as a baseline to measure the impact of future marketing efforts and strategies.

Analyzing Marketing Effectiveness

1. Choose a recent marketing campaign and calculate its ROI. Use the formula:

   ROI = [Net Profit / Total Marketing Investment] × 100

   Analyze the components that contributed to its success or shortcomings, focusing on cost-efficiency and revenue generation.
2. Calculate the Customer Acquisition Cost (CAC) and Customer Lifetime Value (CLTV) for your startup. Assess the ratio between CLTV and CAC to evaluate the sustainability of your marketing investments. Reflect on strategies to improve this ratio by either reducing CAC or enhancing CLTV.
3. Perform an evaluation of your marketing mix to identify which channels and strategies are delivering the best ROI. Consider reallocating resources from lower-performing channels to those with higher returns, experimenting cautiously to validate these decisions.

Refining Strategies for Enhanced ROI

1. Develop a plan for A/B testing different aspects of your marketing strategy. This could involve testing different messaging, channels, targeting criteria, or creative designs. Define clear hypotheses for each test, including expected outcomes and KPIs to measure.
2. Create a systematic approach to integrate customer feedback into your marketing strategy refinement process. This could involve regular customer surveys, feedback forms, or social media listening. Use insights gathered

to inform adjustments in marketing messaging, targeting, and channel selection.

3. Schedule quarterly innovation sprints focused on exploring new marketing strategies, technologies, or channels that have the potential to enhance ROI. Each sprint should result in a set of actionable experiments to be implemented and evaluated in the following quarter.

Challenge For You

Select one marketing channel or campaign with room for improvement in ROI. Utilize the exercises above to redefine objectives, enhance tracking, conduct a detailed performance analysis, and implement strategic adjustments based on your findings. Document the process, results, and learnings from this project, aiming to develop a replicable model for continuous marketing optimization.

Conclusion:

Measuring marketing ROI isn't just about crunching numbers; it's a strategic imperative that informs smarter decisions, better budget allocation, and ultimately, stronger business growth. By focusing on the key metrics that matter, leveraging advanced analytics for deeper insights, and adopting a culture of continuous improvement, entrepreneurs can ensure their marketing efforts are not just effective, but also efficient. As we move forward, the ability to measure, understand, and act on marketing ROI will remain a critical determinant of business success in an ever-evolving market landscape.

In our next exploration, we delve into the power of customer feedback, uncovering how it can be harnessed to refine marketing strategies, enhance product offerings, and elevate the overall customer experience.

11

Marketing Automation and CRM Integration

"The future of marketing is personalization and automation."
— Erik Qualman

I n the rapidly evolving landscape of digital marketing, the integration of marketing automation and CRM systems has emerged as a transformative strategy for businesses aiming to streamline their operations and foster closer connections with their customers. This chapter delves into the heart of how automation tools, when synergistically combined with the insights and organization provided by CRM platforms, can revolutionize marketing efforts. It offers a deep dive into optimizing marketing campaigns, personalizing customer experiences at scale, and ultimately, enhancing the efficiency and efficacy of business strategies. Through this exploration, entrepreneurs will uncover the methodology to leverage these technologies, transforming vast arrays of data into actionable, personalized marketing initiatives that resonate deeply with their target audiences.

The integration of marketing automation and CRM transcends the conventional boundaries of marketing and sales, creating a cohesive ecosystem where customer insights drive targeted actions, and every interaction is an opportunity for data enrichment. This seamless interplay ensures that marketing efforts are not just consistent but also continuously optimized based on a unified view of the customer journey. By automating repetitive tasks and utilizing CRM data to inform and tailor marketing communications, businesses can achieve a level of personalization and efficiency previously unattainable. This chapter provides a blueprint for setting up integrated systems, crafting automated workflows that nurture leads and delight customers, and ultimately, turning these technological investments into significant returns for your business.

Amidst the digital noise, the ability to cut through with messages that not only reach but also resonate with your audience has never been more valuable. Marketing automation and CRM integration stand at the forefront of this challenge, offering a solution that combines the precision of data-driven decision-making with the authenticity of personalized engagement. From selecting the right platforms to mapping out sophisticated customer journeys, this chapter equips you with the knowledge and tools to build a marketing infrastructure that elevates your brand, fosters customer loyalty, and drives sustainable growth.

Opening Anecdote: The HubSpot Revolution

HubSpot has become synonymous with inbound marketing excellence, largely due to its pioneering use of marketing automation and seamless CRM integration. By creating a platform where every marketing action feeds into a rich customer database, HubSpot not only optimized its own marketing strategies but also empowered businesses worldwide to do the same. Their approach demonstrates how integrated systems can transform the marketing landscape, making personalized, data-driven marketing accessible to all.

> **Quick Thought:**
> *Marketing automation and CRM integration bridge the gap between data and action, turning insights into tailored customer interactions that drive engagement and conversion.*

Entrepreneurship in Action: Key Ingredients

- **Seamless Data Flow:** Ensure a fluid exchange of information between your marketing automation tools and CRM system to maintain a unified customer view across all touchpoints.
- **Automated Personalization:** Leverage automation to deliver personalized marketing messages at scale, enhancing customer experiences and increasing the effectiveness of marketing campaigns.
- **Data-Driven Decision Making:** Utilize the comprehensive insights generated by integrated systems to make informed marketing decisions, optimize strategies, and maximize ROI.

Case Study: Mailchimp's Evolution into an All-in-One Marketing Platform

Mailchimp's transformation from a simple email marketing tool to a comprehensive marketing platform illustrates an insightful response to the evolving needs of digital marketing. Recognizing the critical need for businesses to automate and personalize their marketing efforts, Mailchimp expanded its services to offer a seamless, integrated suite of marketing tools.

- **The Vision:** To empower businesses of all sizes with the tools to automate, personalize, and optimize their marketing campaigns, thereby fostering more meaningful connections with their audience.
- **The Challenge:** Adapting to the dynamic landscape of digital marketing, where personalized communication and efficiency are paramount for business growth.
- **The Approach:** Expanding beyond email marketing, Mailchimp integrated CRM functionalities, behavioral targeting, and advanced analytics into its platform. This expansion enables businesses to create targeted, automated campaigns informed by comprehensive customer insights.
- **The Impact:** Mailchimp's strategic growth into a holistic marketing platform has reinforced its leadership in the industry, empowering businesses to streamline their marketing efforts effectively. This evolution has facilitated deeper customer engagement and accelerated growth for a diverse range of businesses, showcasing the value of adaptability and innovation in the digital age.

```
Pro Tip: Start small but think big. Begin with
automating basic marketing tasks and gradually expand
to more complex workflows as you become more
comfortable with the tools and understand your
customers' behaviors better.
```

Exercise: Implementing Marketing Automation and CRM Integration

System Selection and Integration:

1. Evaluate and select marketing automation and CRM platforms that best fit your business needs, considering factors like scalability, ease of use, and integration capabilities.
2. Ensure seamless integration between the two systems for a unified customer data platform.

Automated Workflow Development:

1. Map out key marketing and sales processes that can be automated, such as lead nurturing sequences, customer onboarding emails, and follow-up tasks.
2. Develop automated workflows that trigger based on specific customer behaviors or milestones.

Performance Monitoring and Optimization:

1. Set up metrics and KPIs to measure the effectiveness of

your marketing automation and CRM initiatives.

2. Regularly review performance data to identify areas for improvement, optimize workflows, and refine customer segmentation and targeting strategies.

Challenge For You: Identify a repetitive marketing or sales process in your business that consumes considerable time and resources. Develop an automated workflow to streamline this process, leveraging your CRM data to personalize interactions. Monitor the impact on efficiency and customer response, adjusting the workflow based on feedback and results.

Conclusion:

Marketing automation and CRM integration represent the nexus of modern marketing—where efficiency meets personalization. For entrepreneurs navigating the digital landscape, mastering these tools is not just an advantage; it's a necessity. By automating routine tasks, personalizing customer interactions based on rich data insights, and fostering seamless collaboration between marketing and sales, businesses can unlock unprecedented growth and build lasting customer relationships in an increasingly competitive market.

As we move forward, the fusion of automation and CRM will continue to redefine the marketing paradigm, making it essential for entrepreneurs to stay ahead of the curve, continuously adapt, and leverage these technologies to their fullest potential.

12

Branding and Visual Identity

"Your brand is a story unfolding across all customer touch points."
— Jonah Sachs

I n the labyrinth of the business world, the power of a well-crafted brand and visual identity cannot be overstated. In today's fast-paced and visually driven market, the essence of branding extends far beyond a memorable logo or catchy tagline. It encapsulates the totality of experiences, perceptions, and emotions that people associate with your company and offerings. A compelling brand and visual identity not only distinguish your business in a crowded marketplace but also build a deep, enduring connection with your audience. This chapter explores the transformative power of branding and visual identity, offering a comprehensive guide for entrepreneurs on how to articulate and express their business's unique story and values through design, messaging, and customer experience. It delves into the strategies for creating a brand that resonates on an emotional level, stands out for its distinctiveness, and consistently delivers on its promises across every interaction.

Creating a brand is akin to weaving a tapestry that depicts your company's journey, beliefs, and aspirations. It requires a thoughtful blend of creativity, strategy, and authenticity. Through engaging narratives and a cohesive visual language, a well-crafted brand communicates who you are, what you stand for, and how you're different from competitors. It's about creating a unique identity that speaks to the hearts and minds of your audience, making your business not just seen but felt and remembered. This chapter underscores the importance of a cohesive narrative and visual identity in crafting a brand that captivates and connects, turning passive onlookers into passionate advocates.

As we embark on this exploration, we'll uncover the elements that constitute a powerful brand identity, from the psychology of color and typography to the crafting of a brand story that aligns with your audience's values and aspirations. We'll discuss the role of consistency in building trust and how adaptability within your brand's visual and communicative expressions can foster a lasting relationship with your audience. With practical insights and actionable strategies, this chapter equips you with the tools needed to build a brand that not only stands out but also stands the test of time, driving business growth and fostering customer loyalty.

Opening Anecdote: Apple's Brand Evolution

Apple's journey to becoming a behemoth in technology and design is a testament to the transformative power of branding and visual identity. By marrying innovation with sleek, minimalist design, Apple has created more than products; it has cultivated a lifestyle and a loyal community. Their brand, characterized by the iconic bitten apple and a commitment to "Think Different," showcases how consistent, powerful branding coupled with distinct visual identity can captivate minds and markets alike.

> *Quick Thought:*
> *Branding is the art of becoming knowable, likable, and trustable. It's about crafting a narrative that your audience wants to be part of.*

Entrepreneurship in Action: Key Ingredients

- **Cohesive Narrative:** A brand story that aligns with your audience's values and aspirations can turn customers into advocates.
- **Distinctive Visual Identity:** A unique visual style sets you apart and makes your brand instantly recognizable.
- **Consistent Experience:** Uniformity in your brand's look, feel, and message across all platforms reinforces your brand's identity and values.

Case Study: Airbnb's Branding Revolution

Airbnb's journey from a modest start-up to a global travel and hospitality titan is a testament to the transformative power of branding. By weaving a compelling narrative around belonging and community, Airbnb has not only redefined the essence of travel but has also cultivated a brand that stands for inclusivity and shared experiences.

- **The Vision:** To transform the travel experience into one that fosters a sense of belonging and connection, making every journey an opportunity to live like a local.
- **The Challenge:** Differentiating itself in the crowded and conventional travel industry, Airbnb sought to establish a brand that transcends mere transactions, creating a global community of hosts and travelers.
- **The Approach:** Airbnb unveiled a vibrant visual identity, centered around the "Bélo" logo which embodies belonging. Through storytelling and showcasing real experiences from its community, Airbnb's branding resonates with a sense of adventure and inclusivity.
- **The Impact:** This strategic emphasis on branding has not only elevated Airbnb's position in the travel industry but also forged a loyal global community. Airbnb's success illustrates the profound impact of a coherent and emotionally resonant brand narrative in cultivating loyalty and driving growth.

```
Pro Tip: Flexibility within consistency. While
maintaining a consistent brand image is crucial,
allowing room for flexibility and evolution keeps
your brand relevant and relatable.
```

Exercise: Shaping Your Brand's Legacy

Crafting Your Brand Story

1. Conduct a workshop for your team focused on crafting your brand's narrative. Use storytelling techniques to explore the origins, mission, values, and vision of your brand. Aim to create a story that connects emotionally with your audience, reflecting what you stand for and aspire to achieve.

2. Utilize the Value Proposition Canvas to clearly define the value your brand offers to its customers. This exercise helps in articulating how your products or services solve customer problems or enhance their lives, which is central to your brand story.

3. Create detailed audience personas representing your key customer segments. Include demographics, interests, challenges, and aspirations. Tailor your brand story to address the specific needs and desires of these personas, ensuring relevance and resonance.

Designing Your Visual Identity

1. Compile a mood board that captures the essence of your brand's visual identity. Include colors, typography, imagery, and design elements that align with your brand story and values. This mood board will serve as a reference point for developing your brand's visual assets.

2. Engage in a logo design challenge, either internally with your team or by collaborating with professional designers. Brief the designers on your brand story and visual identity mood board. Review the designs to select a logo that best represents your brand's ethos and appeals to your target audience.

3. Select typography and a color scheme that complement

your logo and are reflective of your brand's personality. Consider the psychological impact of colors and fonts on consumer perception, ensuring they contribute to a cohesive visual identity.

Ensuring Brand Consistency

1. Develop a comprehensive brand style guide detailing the usage of your logo, color scheme, typography, imagery, and other visual elements. This guide should also encompass tone of voice and messaging style, ensuring consistency across all communication channels.
2. Conduct a brand audit across all customer touchpoints, including your website, social media, marketing materials, and packaging. Identify inconsistencies or deviations from your brand style guide and develop a plan to address them.
3. Organize training sessions for your team to ensure everyone understands the importance of brand consistency and knows how to apply the brand style guide. Consider internal branding efforts, such as branded office supplies or team apparel, to reinforce your brand identity within your organization.

Challenge For You

Undertake a brand refresh project if your audit reveals significant inconsistencies or if your current brand identity no longer aligns with your brand story. Focus on updating visual elements, refining your narrative, and enhancing overall brand consistency. Implement the changes across all platforms and materials, measuring audience response to gauge the impact of your refresh.

Conclusion:

A strong brand and visual identity are invaluable assets in the entrepreneurial arsenal. They are not merely tools for differentiation but are the very essence of how your business is perceived and experienced. By crafting a cohesive narrative and distinctive visual style, and ensuring consistency across all interactions, entrepreneurs can forge a brand that not only captures attention but also wins hearts and minds. As we move forward, remember that your brand is an evolving story, one that requires care, attention, and strategic thinking to truly flourish in the competitive business landscape.

13

Customer Retention and Upselling

"The purpose of a business is to create a customer who creates customers."
— Shiv Singh

I n the intricate dance of business growth, the spotlight often shines on customer acquisition, yet the true performance lies in the ability to retain those customers and enhance their value over time. The art of retaining customers and strategically enhancing their lifetime value through upselling is not merely a tactic but a critical component of sustainable business growth. This chapter explores the nuanced strategies behind nurturing lasting customer relationships, highlighting how businesses can elevate initial transactions to long-term loyalty. With a focus on understanding and anticipating customer needs, creating value-driven loyalty programs, and adopting ethical upselling practices, entrepreneurs are equipped to not only retain their customer base but also to increase their spending over time.

Delving into the psychology of customer loyalty, this chapter emphasizes the importance of viewing every customer interaction as an opportunity to reinforce trust, deliver exceptional value, and solidify the customer's commitment to the brand. It presents actionable insights on crafting customized experiences that resonate with the unique needs and preferences of your audience, thereby fostering a sense of belonging and loyalty. From implementing innovative loyalty programs that reward customers in meaningful ways to personalizing communications and offers based on deep data insights, the strategies outlined here aim to transform the conventional customer journey into a dynamic, engaging experience that encourages repeat business and referrals.

Moreover, this chapter addresses the strategic nuances of upselling, underscoring the significance of aligning additional offers with the customer's evolving needs and aspirations. By presenting upselling as a natural extension of the customer's journey with your brand, businesses can enhance the perceived value of their offerings, ensuring that customers feel understood and appreciated rather than pressured. Through real-world examples and case studies, we illustrate the transformative impact of well-executed customer retention and upselling strategies on business growth, customer satisfaction, and brand advocacy.

Opening Anecdote: The Sephora Loyalty Program

Sephora's Beauty Insider loyalty program exemplifies the profound impact of customer retention strategies. By rewarding purchases with points redeemable for premium products and exclusive experiences, Sephora has cultivated a community of beauty enthusiasts who are not just buyers but passionate brand advocates. This program demonstrates how understanding and catering to customer desires can transform satisfaction into loyalty.

> ### Quick Thought:
> *Customer retention is not merely about keeping customers; it's about deepening the relationship, making each interaction a stepping stone to greater loyalty and value.*

Entrepreneurship in Action: Key Ingredients

- **Understanding Customer Needs:** Dive deep into the preferences and behaviors of your customers to tailor experiences that resonate and add value.
- **Rewarding Loyalty:** Implement programs that acknowledge and reward customer loyalty, turning satisfaction into advocacy and repeat business.
- **Strategic Upselling:** Approach upselling as an opportunity to enhance the customer's experience, offering solutions that genuinely meet their evolving needs.

Case Study: Netflix's Personalized Recommendations

Netflix, the pioneering streaming service, has set the gold standard in harnessing the power of big data to transform viewer engagement through personalized content recommendations. Recognizing the diverse palette of global audiences, Netflix embarked on a mission to create a deeply personalized viewing experience, ensuring that every interaction with the platform feels intuitively tailored to individual preferences.

- **The Vision:** To revolutionize the viewing experience by curating content that resonates with the unique preferences of each subscriber, thereby transforming passive viewing into an engaging discovery journey.
- **The Challenge:** Amidst an ever-expanding library of content, the challenge was to develop a system that accurately predicts and presents content that aligns with the varied tastes of millions of subscribers worldwide.
- **The Strategy:** Netflix's approach was to employ sophisticated machine learning algorithms that meticulously analyze viewing habits, including what, when, and how subscribers watch. This data-driven strategy enables Netflix to craft and deliver highly personalized recommendations, aiming to captivate audiences with content that speaks directly to their interests and viewing history.
- **The Impact:** The implementation of this personalized recommendation system has been a game-changer for Netflix, significantly reducing subscriber churn and reinforcing its dominance in the competitive streaming market. By prioritizing personalization, Netflix has not only enhanced subscriber satisfaction but also underscored the transformative potential of leveraging big data for customer retention and engagement.

Netflix's mastery of personalized recommendations exemplifies the synergy between technology and entertainment, showcasing how data-driven personalization can create a unique and engaging consumer experience that stands out in the crowded digital landscape.

```
Pro Tip: Listen and adapt. The key to successful
customer retention and upselling lies in being
attuned to customer feedback and ready to evolve your
offerings in response to their needs.
```

Exercise: Building Enduring Customer Relationships

Crafting Loyalty Programs

1. Host a workshop with your team to brainstorm ideas for a loyalty program that aligns with your brand values and appeals to your customer base. Consider different models, such as points-based systems, tiered rewards, or membership clubs. Define the structure, rewards, and criteria for participation.
2. Before finalizing your loyalty program, gather feedback from a segment of your customer base. Use surveys, focus groups, or one-on-one interviews to understand their preferences and expectations from such a program. Incorporate this feedback to refine your loyalty program, ensuring it meets customer desires.
3. Develop a detailed plan for launching your loyalty program, including communication strategies, enrollment processes, and tracking mechanisms. Outline how you will measure the program's success in terms of enrollment rates, customer engagement, and impact on retention.

Personalizing Customer Experiences

1. Conduct an audit of your current capabilities in collecting and utilizing customer data for personalization. Identify gaps in data collection, integration, and analysis. Plan enhancements to your CRM system or other tools to improve personalization across customer touchpoints.
2. Use customer data to create detailed segments based on purchasing behavior, preferences, or engagement levels. Develop targeted communication strategies for each segment, focusing on personalized messages, offers, and recommendations that cater to their specific interests.
3. Select one customer segment and design an experiment to test the effectiveness of personalized experiences. This could involve customized product recommendations, tailored email marketing, or personalized offers. Measure the impact on customer engagement, retention, and upselling success.

Mastering Upselling Techniques

1. Analyze your product or service offerings to identify potential upselling opportunities. Look for natural complements or premium versions that could enhance the customer's experience. Understand the value proposition of each upsell to effectively communicate its benefits to customers.
2. Train your sales and customer service teams on ethical upselling techniques. Emphasize the importance of understanding customer needs, offering relevant solutions, and avoiding aggressive sales tactics. Role-playing exercises

can be useful for practicing upselling in a customer-centric manner.

3. Implement tracking mechanisms to monitor the success of your upselling strategies. Set KPIs such as upsell conversion rates, average order value increase, and customer satisfaction scores. Use this data to refine your upselling approaches continuously.

Challenge For You

Choose a customer journey stage with potential for improved retention or upselling (e.g., post-purchase follow-up, renewal phase). Design and implement targeted initiatives to enhance the customer experience at this stage, incorporating loyalty program elements, personalization, and ethical upselling tactics. Measure the impact on customer loyalty, repeat purchases, and overall satisfaction.

Conclusion:

The journey from attracting to retaining customers is filled with opportunities to deepen connections and enhance value. Through thoughtful engagement, personalized experiences, and strategic upselling, entrepreneurs can build a loyal customer base that not only drives current profitability but also lays the foundation for sustainable growth. Remember, in the realm of business, the most successful stories are those where customers become the champions of your brand, inspired not just to stay but to bring others into the fold.

14

International Marketing and Localization

"Globalization means we all need to be more sensitive to the cultural nuances of our diverse audiences."
— Ann Handley

Venturing into international markets is a bold step toward unlocking new levels of growth and exposure for any entrepreneurial endeavor. This chapter serves as a compass for navigating the complexities of international marketing and localization, offering essential strategies for entrepreneurs who aim to transcend domestic borders and connect with customers across the globe. It emphasizes the importance of understanding cultural nuances, tailoring marketing efforts to diverse audiences, and the strategic role of localization in building a global brand presence.

As businesses seek to carve out their niche in the global market, the challenge extends beyond simple translation of content; it requires a deep, empathetic understanding of local cultures, preferences, and consumer behavior. This chapter explores how to adeptly marry your core brand identity with the unique characteristics of each target market, ensuring that your brand not only enters new markets but thrives in them. It delves into practical steps for adapting products, messages, and marketing tactics to resonate with local audiences, all while maintaining the universal appeal of your brand.

This exploration into international marketing and localization is underscored by real-world examples and actionable insights, designed to equip entrepreneurs with the tools they need to successfully expand their business horizons. From conducting market research and developing a localization strategy to executing tailored marketing campaigns and measuring their impact, this chapter lays out a comprehensive roadmap for global brand expansion. Through a blend of strategic thinking and creative adaptation, entrepreneurs are guided on how to make their mark on the world stage, turning the challenge of cultural diversity into a competitive advantage.

Opening Anecdote: Rakuten's Embrace of Englishnization

Rakuten, Japan's largest e-commerce site, embarked on an ambitious journey to globalize its operations by adopting English as its official language of business—a strategy dubbed "Englishnization." This bold move by CEO Hiroshi Mikitani was not just about language; it was a strategic pivot towards creating a unified corporate culture that could thrive in the global market. By embracing Englishnization, Rakuten tore down linguistic barriers within its organization, fostering better communication, innovation, and a stronger presence on the international stage. This initiative highlights the significance of cultural adaptation and the foresight required to navigate the complexities of global markets.

> ***Quick Thought:***
> *Effective international marketing isn't just about reaching global audiences; it's about connecting with them in a way that feels both universal and personal.*

Entrepreneurship in Action: Key Ingredients

- **Cultural Intelligence:** Develop a deep understanding of the cultural nuances, preferences, and values of each target market to ensure your marketing strategies are respectful and relevant.
- **Adaptive Branding:** While maintaining your brand's core identity, be flexible in adapting visual and messaging elements to align with local expectations and sensibilities.
- **Localized Engagement:** Utilize local channels and platforms for marketing communication to engage with audiences in the most direct and authentic manner possible.

Case Study: Xiaomi's Global Expansion Strategy

Xiaomi's ascent to a global powerhouse in the electronics market underscores a strategic masterclass in understanding and adapting to the nuanced landscape of international markets. Originating as a brand celebrated for its high-quality, yet affordable smartphones, Xiaomi diverged from its online-only sales model to embrace local partnerships and physical retail strategies tailored to each new market it entered. This flexibility allowed Xiaomi to navigate and thrive within diverse consumer ecosystems.

- **The Vision:** To democratize technology worldwide by offering cutting-edge, affordable electronics, tailored to meet the specific needs and preferences of consumers across different regions.
- **The Challenge:** Breaking into and gaining a foothold in the highly competitive global smartphone and consumer electronics markets, each with its own distinct consumer behaviors and expectations.
- **The Approach:** Xiaomi's strategy was multi-faceted, focusing on local market insights to adapt its product offerings and sales strategies. In India, Xiaomi crafted products with local consumers in mind, leveraging social media influencers and community events to build brand loyalty. Furthermore, Xiaomi customized its MIUI operating system with regional languages and services, enhancing the user experience through personalization.
- **The Impact:** Through its adept adaptation and community-focused marketing, Xiaomi quickly ascended to become a leading brand in various key markets, including India and Indonesia. Its success is a testament to the efficacy of localizing products and marketing strategies to resonate with the target audience, underscoring the significance of cultural sensitivity and engagement in global expansion efforts.

Pro Tip: Localization is a dialogue. Engage with
local experts, communities, and customers to
continually refine your approach and ensure your
brand remains as locally relevant as it is globally
recognizable.

Exercise: Crafting Your Global Strategy

Understanding and Analyzing Target Markets

1. Identify and research three potential international markets for your product or service. Analyze demographic, economic, and cultural factors that could influence market entry. Summarize your findings and rank these markets based on their attractiveness and fit for your business.
2. Organize a workshop for your team that focuses on building cultural competency for your chosen international markets. Include sessions on local customs, business practices, communication styles, and consumer behavior. Invite cultural experts or use online resources to facilitate learning.
3. For each identified market, conduct a detailed analysis of the competitive landscape. Identify local and international competitors, their market positioning, and strategies. Use this information to pinpoint opportunities and challenges for your brand's entry.

Developing a Localization Strategy

1. Create a blueprint for adapting your brand's visual identity and messaging to align with each target market's cultural nuances. This should include variations in logo, color scheme, taglines, and overall brand persona. Ensure that core brand values are maintained while making necessary adjustments.

2. Host a brainstorming session to explore adaptations to your product or service that may be required to meet local preferences or regulatory requirements. Consider features, packaging, or additional services that could enhance local appeal and usability.

3. Draft a plan for localizing your marketing content, including websites, social media, advertising, and customer support materials. Detail the translation process, cultural adaptation, and the selection of local images or references to ensure relevance and engagement.

Executing and Refining Your International Approach

1. Identify potential local partners, such as distributors, influencers, or business associations, that can aid in your market entry. Outline strategies for engaging and establishing mutually beneficial partnerships to facilitate local market penetration.

2. Plan and execute a pilot marketing campaign in one of your target markets. Use localized content and tailored marketing channels to reach your audience. Set clear objectives and metrics to measure campaign performance.

3. Establish a system for collecting and analyzing feedback from your international customers. Use this feedback to make iterative improvements to your products, marketing

strategies, and overall approach to localization.

Challenge For You

Choose one of the markets you've analyzed and develop a comprehensive action plan for market entry. This should include detailed strategies for localization, partnership development, marketing execution, and feedback incorporation. Implement your plan, monitor its effectiveness, and adjust based on real-time market feedback and performance metrics.

Conclusion:

Embarking on the journey of international marketing and localization is both a challenge and an opportunity. By embracing the diversity of global markets and committing to genuine localization efforts, entrepreneurs can unlock new avenues for growth, engagement, and brand loyalty. Remember, in the global village of today's economy, the ability to communicate with respect and understanding across cultures is not just an advantage; it's a necessity. The path forward is paved with the insights gained from every market interaction, guiding your business towards international success and beyond.

In our exploration, we've uncovered the foundational strategies that enable businesses to thrive on the global stage. As we look ahead, the ongoing evolution of markets and consumer preferences will demand agility, foresight, and an unwavering commitment to delivering value that transcends geographical and cultural boundaries.

15

Emerging Marketing Trends and Future Outlook

"Adaptability is about the powerful difference between adapting to cope and adapting to win."
— Max McKeown

As the digital landscape unfurls with unprecedented speed, marketers stand at the frontier, deciphering emerging trends and technologies that reshape how we connect with our audience. In an era defined by rapid technological advancements and shifting consumer behaviors, the ability to anticipate and adapt to emerging marketing trends is not merely an advantage—it's imperative for survival and success. This chapter propels entrepreneurs into the future of marketing, dissecting trends that are set to shape the digital and physical marketplaces. It equips readers with foresight and strategies to harness these trends, ensuring their marketing efforts remain innovative, relevant, and effective in captivating their target audience. This journey into the future is not just about predicting changes; it's about preparing to lead through them.

The chapter emphasizes the fusion of technology and personalization, illustrating how advancements such as artificial intelligence, augmented reality, and machine learning are redefining the ways in which brands engage with their audiences. It explores the evolving landscape of consumer expectations, where personalized experiences and authentic brand interactions become the benchmarks for excellence. Through a blend of analytical insights and creative strategies, the chapter guides entrepreneurs on leveraging these technological tools to create marketing campaigns that are not only targeted and efficient but also deeply resonant with consumers on a personal level.

Furthermore, the narrative of this chapter underscores the importance of agility in marketing strategy development. It advocates for a proactive approach to embracing new platforms, experimenting with novel content formats, and engaging in dynamic storytelling methods. This adaptability is presented as crucial for navigating the fluidity of consumer interests and the ever-expanding digital ecosystem. By integrating case studies and actionable exercises, the chapter offers a comprehensive toolkit for entrepreneurs to innovate their marketing practices, ensuring they can effectively communicate their brand's story and value proposition in an increasingly competitive landscape.

Opening Anecdote:

Rent the Runway's Fashion Forward Thinking

Rent the Runway has revolutionized the fashion industry by introducing an innovative model that blends sustainability with luxury. Founded by Jennifer Hyman and Jennifer Fleiss, this pioneering service allows customers to rent high-end fashion items rather than purchasing them, addressing both environmental concerns and the desire for variety and exclusivity in fashion. This approach not only highlights the evolving consumer preferences towards sustainable and circular economies but also demonstrates how understanding and adapting to these shifts can create new market opportunities and redefine traditional industries.

> **Quick Thought:**
> *The future of marketing lies in the ability to foresee changes, harness new technologies, and craft messages that resonate on a deeply personal level with the audience.*

Entrepreneurship in Action: Key Ingredients

- **Technological Agility:** Embrace new technologies that enhance customer understanding and engagement, from AI to AR, positioning your brand at the cutting edge of innovation.
- **Authentic Engagement:** Forge genuine connections with your audience, leveraging influencers, user-generated content, and transparent communication to build trust and loyalty.
- **Adaptive Strategies:** Stay nimble, ready to pivot your marketing strategies in response to emerging trends, consumer behaviors, and technological advancements.

Case Study: Slack's Strategic Market Entry

Slack redefined business communication by seamlessly integrating into the daily workflows of modern teams. Its market entry wasn't just about launching a new product; it was about introducing a revolution in collaboration. By keenly understanding the evolving needs of contemporary workplaces, Slack offered an innovative, intuitive solution that quickly became indispensable for enhancing productivity and fostering team unity.

The Vision: To transform the landscape of team communication by creating a platform that not only meets the immediate needs of modern workplaces but also anticipates future challenges in collaboration.

The Challenge: In a market cluttered with traditional communication tools, Slack's challenge was to stand out—not just as a new option, but as a necessary evolution for improving team dynamics and efficiency. The goal was to shift the perception of workplace communication from a routine task to an engaging, seamless experience.

The Strategy:

- **Organic Growth through Authentic Engagement:** Slack chose to eschew conventional marketing in favor of organic growth, propelled by word-of-mouth endorsements from early adopters. This approach leveraged the power of genuine user satisfaction and network effects to spread awareness.

- **Freemium Model to Demonstrate Value:** By adopting a freemium model, Slack allowed users to witness firsthand the platform's potential to revolutionize their communication, ensuring that financial commitment came after users were convinced of the value.

- **Continuous Improvement through User Feedback:** Slack's commitment to excellence was evident in its meticulous collection and incorporation of user feedback. This continuous loop of feedback and improvement ensured that Slack not only met but exceeded user expectations, fostering a deeply loyal user base.

The Impact: Slack's user-centric approach catalyzed its transformation from a newcomer to a dominant force in business communication. Its success story is a testament to the power of aligning product innovation with user needs and the unparalleled value of community and customer-focused growth strategies. Through understanding and addressing common workplace communication challenges, Slack not only captured but also expanded its market, setting new standards for productivity and collaboration tools worldwide.

Reflection: Slack's strategic market entry showcases the importance of empathy in innovation. By focusing on the human elements of business—connection, communication, and collaboration—Slack didn't just create a product; it sparked a movement towards more dynamic, inclusive, and efficient workplaces.

```
Pro Tip: Keep the human element central. As digital
tools and platforms evolve, the most successful
marketing strategies will be those that use
technology to amplify, not replace, the human touch.
```

Exercise: Navigating Future Marketing Trends

Exploring New Technologies

1. Dedicate time each month to research emerging technologies with potential marketing applications, such as AI-driven analytics, AR/VR experiences, or blockchain for customer loyalty programs. Compile a report on how these technologies could be integrated into your marketing strategies, including potential benefits and challenges.

2. Choose one technology identified in your research as promising and develop a pilot project to test its effectiveness in a real-world marketing scenario. Outline objectives, implementation steps, expected outcomes, and metrics for success. Analyze the results to determine scalability and integration into broader marketing efforts.

3. Organize a workshop for your marketing and product development teams to brainstorm innovative uses of new technologies in your marketing initiatives. Focus on creating a culture of continuous innovation, encouraging team members to think creatively about leveraging tech trends to enhance customer engagement and brand differentiation.

Enhancing Community Engagement

1. Draft a blueprint for building or enhancing your brand community. This should include strategies for engaging with your audience on social media, forums, or brand-owned platforms, fostering user-generated content, and

encouraging customer feedback and interaction.

2. Identify influencers or key opinion leaders within your industry who align with your brand values. Initiate a collaboration on a small-scale marketing initiative designed to increase brand visibility and community engagement. Evaluate the effectiveness based on engagement metrics and feedback.

3. Launch a co-creation challenge inviting customers to contribute ideas for new products, services, or marketing campaigns. Promote the challenge across your communication channels, offering incentives for participation. Use this initiative to deepen customer involvement and gather innovative ideas.

Perfecting Personalization Techniques

1. Conduct an audit of your current capabilities in personalizing marketing communications. Identify areas for improvement and invest in tools or processes that allow for more granular data analysis and customer segmentation.

2. Using insights from your audit, design a hyper-personalized marketing campaign targeting a specific customer segment. Include personalized offers, content, and messaging based on customer behavior and preferences. Measure the campaign's success through engagement rates and conversion metrics.

3. Establish a system for collecting and analyzing customer feedback on personalized experiences. Use this feedback to continuously refine and improve personalization techniques, ensuring they remain relevant and effective as

customer preferences evolve.

Challenge For You

Identify a marketing trend or technology that is just beginning to emerge but has the potential to significantly impact your industry. Develop a comprehensive plan to incorporate this trend into your marketing strategy, focusing on long-term goals and the anticipated evolution of customer preferences. Implement a scaled-down version of this plan as a test, collecting data on its performance and scalability.

Conclusion:

In navigating the future of marketing, the ability to anticipate changes, engage deeply with consumers, and innovate boldly will distinguish the leaders from the followers. Rent the Runway and Slack exemplify how aligning with consumer values and leveraging technology can redefine industries and drive success. As we move forward, let these examples inspire you to explore new horizons, stay agile, and remain committed to delivering value and relevance in an ever-evolving market landscape.

16

Leveraging AI for Entrepreneurial Success: Empowering Entrepreneurs with Dynamic Prompts

"Artificial Intelligence is a tool, not a threat. When used wisely, it can be the entrepreneur's best friend."
— Reid Hoffman

The integration of Artificial Intelligence (AI) into the entrepreneurial landscape marks a revolution in how businesses conceive, strategize, and execute their visions. Artificial Intelligence (AI) emerges not just as a technological innovation but as a pivotal force reshaping the business landscape. This transformative era, marked by AI's integration into various facets of business operations, offers unprecedented opportunities for growth, efficiency, and personalization. In this last chapter, let's embarks on a comprehensive exploration of leveraging AI to amplify entrepreneurial endeavors, providing a deep dive into dynamic prompts powered by AI models like ChatGPT that can revolutionize how entrepreneurs approach problem-solving, innovation, and customer engagement.

The chapter elucidates the transformative potential of AI in crafting bespoke solutions, enhancing decision-making processes, and fostering intimate connections with audiences at scale. It navigates through practical applications of AI, from generating insightful articles and sophisticated business plans to developing strategic marketing materials and pitch decks. By harnessing the power of AI, entrepreneurs can not only streamline their operations but also unlock creative potentials that were previously unimaginable, propelling their ventures into new heights of success.

Moreover, this chapter addresses the critical aspect of integrating AI into the entrepreneurial strategy with precision and intentionality. It emphasizes the importance of clear, targeted prompts that guide AI to generate outputs aligning with specific business objectives, thereby ensuring that AI serves as a catalyst for innovation rather than a mere tool for automation. Through real-world anecdotes and actionable exercises, the chapter equips entrepreneurs with the knowledge and skills to harness AI's capabilities effectively, navigating the intricacies of AI-driven strategies to foster growth, enhance customer experiences, and maintain a competitive edge in the fast-evolving business world.

Opening Anecdote: Duolingo's AI-Driven Language Learning

Duolingo's rise to prominence in the language learning domain is a compelling testament to AI's transformative potential. By leveraging AI to personalize learning experiences, Duolingo has not only democratized language education but also significantly enhanced user engagement and retention. This narrative illustrates the profound impact that AI can have in tailoring services to meet individual needs and preferences, setting a new standard for personalized user experiences.

> **Quick Thought:**
> *AI's true power for entrepreneurs lies in its ability to transform vast data into actionable insights, personalized experiences, and innovative solutions.*

Harnessing AI's Power: A Multifaceted Approach

The dawn of AI, particularly models like ChatGPT, marks a pivotal shift in how entrepreneurs approach problem-solving, innovation, and customer engagement. Herein lies a guide to leveraging AI's prowess through dynamic prompts, categorized to address various entrepreneurial needs:

Informative Articles

- **Prompt for Business Strategies**: "Generate an article outlining innovative business strategies for digital startups in emerging markets."
- **Marketing Techniques Insight**: "Create a detailed guide

on integrating traditional and digital marketing techniques for maximum outreach."

Business Plans

- **Executive Summary Assistance**: "Help draft an executive summary that captures a sustainable business model for a tech startup."
- **Market Analysis Guide**: "Provide a step-by-step guide for conducting a comprehensive market analysis for an e-commerce venture."

Marketing Materials

- **Website Content Creation**: "Suggest engaging content for the home page of a sustainable fashion brand's website."
- **Email Campaign Strategies**: "Draft an email for a campaign aimed at re-engaging dormant subscribers for a SaaS platform."

Pitch Decks

- **Market Opportunity Slide**: "Assist in creating a slide highlighting the market opportunity for renewable energy solutions."
- **Financial Projections Advice**: "Offer guidance on presenting financial projections in a pitch deck for a fintech startup."

Problem-solving and Decision-making

- **Pricing Strategy Dilemmas**: "Advise on effective pricing strategies for a premium lifestyle product in a competitive market."
- **Customer Retention Solutions**: "Suggest innovative strategies for improving customer retention in the mobile app industry."

Entrepreneurial Advice and Tips

- **Networking Strategies**: "Provide tips for effective networking in virtual conferences for early-stage entrepreneurs."
- **Time Management Techniques**: "List top time management hacks for solo entrepreneurs juggling multiple roles."

Market Research Insights

- **Consumer Behavior Trends**: "Summarize key trends in consumer behavior post-pandemic for the retail sector."
- **Competitive Analysis Framework**: "Explain how to conduct a competitive analysis for a new café in a high-traffic area."

Business Strategy Development

- **Growth Hacking Methods**: "Detail growth hacking techniques for SaaS businesses looking to rapidly expand their user base."
- **International Expansion Considerations**: "Discuss key

considerations for a beauty brand planning to expand into Asian markets."

Legal and Regulatory Guidance

- **E-commerce Compliance Checklist**: "List the legal and regulatory compliance checks for launching an e-commerce platform."
- **Intellectual Property Strategy**: "Explain the process of securing patents for a new software product in the tech industry."

Technology and Innovation Insights

- **Blockchain Opportunities**: "Describe potential applications of blockchain technology in enhancing supply chain transparency."
- **AI Integration Best Practices**: "Outline best practices for integrating AI into customer service operations for online retailers."

Pro Tip: Embrace AI as a partner in creativity. Use it to explore new ideas, test hypotheses quickly, and gain insights that would take much longer to uncover manually. The key is to guide AI with specific, targeted prompts that align with your strategic objectives.

Exercise: Crafting Your AI Strategy

Identifying Opportunities for AI Integration:

1. Assess your business operations to identify areas where AI can enhance efficiency, such as customer service or inventory management.
2. Explore AI applications relevant to your industry and how they can be adapted to your specific business needs.

Developing AI-Driven Solutions:

1. Brainstorm innovative ways to incorporate AI into your product offerings or services to provide added value to your customers.
2. Consider AI tools that can improve decision-making, such as predictive analytics or market trend analysis.

Enhancing Customer Engagement with AI:

1. Utilize AI to personalize customer interactions on your digital platforms, tailoring recommendations and content to individual user preferences.
2. Implement AI-powered chatbots to provide instant support and engage customers in meaningful conversations.

Challenge For You: Choose one aspect of your business where AI can make a significant impact. Develop a small pilot project to implement an AI solution in that area, such as a chatbot for customer service or an AI tool for personalized marketing. Monitor the results, gather feedback, and evaluate the potential for broader implementation.

Utilizing AI for Entrepreneurial Growth

This chapter underscores AI's role as an indispensable ally for entrepreneurs. By engaging with AI through thoughtfully crafted prompts, entrepreneurs can unlock tailored advice, strategic insights, and innovative solutions across the spectrum of business activities. Whether it's refining your marketing strategy, exploring new market opportunities, or navigating the complexities of legal compliance, AI stands ready to empower your entrepreneurial journey with knowledge, creativity, and efficiency.

Conclusion

As we look to the future, the synergy between entrepreneurial vision and AI's capabilities will undoubtedly spawn new paradigms of innovation and success. Entrepreneurs who adeptly harness this synergy will not only accelerate their growth but also contribute to shaping a future where businesses thrive on intelligence, adaptability, and a deep understanding of the human experience they seek to enhance.

In this era of rapid technological advancement and ever-evolving market landscapes, let AI be your navigator, guiding your entrepreneurial ship through uncharted waters to shores brimming with opportunity, growth, and unparalleled success.

Epilogue: Mastering Modern Marketing Strategies - Reflecting on "Sales and Scale"

As we conclude our journey through "Sales and Scale: The Entrepreneur's Blueprint for Mastering Marketing and Achieving Explosive Growth," it's clear that the landscape of marketing and sales is both vast and intricately detailed. From the foundational aspects of understanding target markets to the nuanced art of brand storytelling and the strategic execution of digital campaigns, this volume has served as a comprehensive guide to navigating the complexities of modern marketing.

Reflecting on the promises made at the beginning of this guide, we've endeavored to demystify the often intimidating world of marketing and sales, providing you with practical tools, insights, and strategies to identify and connect with your target audience deeply.. Through the exploration of comprehensive market research techniques, the creation of detailed buyer personas, and the crafting of compelling brand stories, we've laid the groundwork for building a robust marketing framework.

Ensuring the Guide's Promises Are Fulfilled

Our journey has equipped you with the knowledge to develop an integrated marketing strategy, utilizing the power of digital platforms to enhance your brand's presence and visibility. We've delved into the secrets behind effective customer acquisition, innovative sales techniques, and the cultivation of meaningful customer relationships, all aimed at fostering loyalty and driving sustainable growth.

Key Takeaways and Application

- **Integrated Marketing Strategy:** We've explored how to weave together various marketing channels and tactics into a cohesive strategy that captivates and engages your audience, driving them towards your desired action.
- **Effective Sales Techniques:** The guide has highlighted tailored sales approaches that resonate with specific customer segments, ensuring that your sales efforts are both efficient and impactful.
- **Cultivating Customer Loyalty:** Through the chapters, we've emphasized the importance of building lasting relationships with your customers, turning satisfied buyers into loyal advocates for your brand.

Challenge for Entrepreneurs

As you stand on the precipice of your entrepreneurial journey, armed with the insights and strategies from "Sales and Scale," the challenge now is to apply these lessons to your unique business context. The path to mastering marketing and achieving explosive growth is both a science and an art, requiring a blend of analytical rigor and creative flair.

Final Reflections

"Sales and Scale" has aimed to transform you into a marketing maestro and sales supremo, equipped to navigate the challenges of the modern marketplace and steer your startup towards unprecedented success. The journey doesn't end here; the world of marketing is ever-evolving, with new trends, technologies, and customer behaviors emerging continually. Staying agile, curious, and committed to learning will be key to scaling new heights and achieving your entrepreneurial dreams.

As we close this chapter and the book, remember that the essence of marketing is about connecting with people — understanding their needs, desires, and aspirations, and finding innovative ways to meet them. With "Sales and Scale" as your guide, you're well on your way to making those connections, crafting memorable experiences, and leaving a lasting impact on your customers and the world.

Let's ignite your entrepreneurial journey together — it's time to scale to new heights!

The Ask

Dear Visionary Entrepreneur,

As we conclude our journey through "Sales and Scale," I hope it has sparked your imagination and armed you with the tools to thrive in marketing and sales. This guide was designed to be your compass, guiding you through the challenges and opportunities of entrepreneurship.

If this book has illuminated your path, please share your experience with a review on Amazon. Your insights help light the way for fellow entrepreneurs, contributing to our shared journey towards innovation and success.

For continued exploration and growth, visit my Amazon author page (https://www.amazon.com/author/patrickhperrine). Together, let's build a future rich with opportunity and achievement.

With immense appreciation for your trust and companionship on this exhilarating voyage,
Patrick H. Perrine

About the Author

Patrick H. Perrine is a trailblazing author, mentor, and seasoned entrepreneur with a spirit that exemplifies the essence of entrepreneurship. From his humble beginnings as a paperboy in Minnesota to his emergence as a globally recognized industry leader, his journey epitomizes resilience and determination.

Fueled by an insatiable thirst for knowledge, Patrick opted for university over his senior high school year, setting the stage for his relentless pursuit of personal growth. His tenure with Up-Start, an organization championing educational opportunities for first-generation Americans, ignited his lifelong commitment to empowering others, extending beyond business and into his early philanthropic endeavors.

In his twenties, Patrick served as a Founding Board member for The Point Foundation, the largest LGBTQ scholarship foundation today. His dedication to fostering inclusivity and aiding LGBTQ students in higher education continues to positively impact hundreds of lives.

Patrick's entrepreneurial journey took flight with myPartner.com, an online dating service that addressed a critical gap in the market. Recognized as one of the "Best Matchmakers" and "Most Innovative Online Dating Sites" by the iDate Industry, the venture earned a Certificate of Recognition issued by California Legislature Assemblyman Mark Leno. This marked Patrick's first step in a journey filled with identifying unique opportunities and delivering transformative solutions across industries from skincare to dog tech.

Despite the hurdles encountered, Patrick's determination only amplified. His passion for nurturing startups led him to establish Rincon Hill Advisors. During this period, he served as a Steering Committee member for StartOut, a leading nonprofit fostering queer entrepreneurship, and consulted with Fortune 500 companies like Berkshire Hathaway and Intuit.

Adding to his achievements as an entrepreneur, Patrick became an angel investor. His foresight led him to invest in promising startups like MisterB&B, the world's largest gay hotelier, and Roadster, the leading commerce platform for car buying. His dog tech venture, too, gained recognition, leading to his selection as a NGLCC Pitch Finalist and participant in the Seamless IoT Accelerator, earning a $100,000 investment offer as a program graduate.

Most recently, Patrick served as an Entrepreneur in Residence (EiR) with 500 StartUps, an organization committed to uplifting global economies through entrepreneurship. This role solidified his dedication to guiding and uplifting aspiring entrepreneurs.

With multiple books to his credit, including recent works "Fail Fast, Recover Faster", "Ignite Your Dream", and "Fueling the Fire," Patrick continues to share his journey and insights. His writing reflects his unwavering commitment to guiding entrepreneurs through their unique journeys.

Patrick H. Perrine is more than a summary of his accomplishments. He stands as a testament to the power of determination, innovation, and a generous spirit. His contributions have been acknowledged in global press publications such as Forbes, Advocate, and Mirror, but his most profound impact lies in the lives of the entrepreneurs he's guided, inspired, and empowered. As he continues sharing his wisdom in the 10 volume series "Be A Unicorn: The New Entrepreneur's Ultimate Guide to Success," Patrick personifies the quintessential entrepreneurial journey—one of resilience, innovation, and the relentless pursuit of personal growth.

Subscribe to my newsletter:

✉ https://patrickperrine.com

Also by Patrick H. Perrine

Your next adventure in entrepreneurship awaits! Choose your guidebook on Amazon (https://www.amazon.com/author/patrickhperrine) or **www.PatrickPerrine.com**, and ignite the spark that takes your venture to new heights. The future is yours to shape!

Unicorn Rising: Ascending to the Pinnacle of Entrepreneurship and the Billionaire's Club

Fueled by entrepreneurial dreams and the allure of the Unicorn Club? Patrick H. Perrine is your guide, offering an unparalleled roadmap set to be every entrepreneur's playbook.

"Unicorn Rising" emerges as the cornerstone of the *Be A Unicorn* series, laying the groundwork that "Sales and Scale" and the other nine volumes build upon.

This seminal work provides an in-depth exploration into the entrepreneurial journey, offering a comprehensive roadmap for those aiming to scale their ventures to the heights of the Unicorn Club.

Driven by the dream of entrepreneurial excellence and a place in the Unicorn Club? Patrick H. Perrine offers an unmatched guide, positioning this book as the ultimate playbook for entrepreneurs.

Within "Unicorn Rising," readers will find a guide not just to achieving lofty valuations, but to navigating the realms of innovation, transformative leadership, and enduring success. It offers insights into the nuances of leadership, the forefront of emerging technologies, financial mastery, and the core of impactful entrepreneurship.

This series acknowledges the uniqueness of each entrepreneurial journey. Patrick delivers foundational wisdom alongside practical tools, emphasizing the tailored path each startup must navigate. Whether you're just beginning your entrepreneurial quest or are a seasoned professional fine-tuning your strategy, this book, and its series, light the way.

Step forward, challenge the status quo, and with "Unicorn Rising," ascend to unprecedented heights in your entrepreneurial venture.

Ignite Your Dream: The Quintessential Checklist for Aspiring Entrepreneurs
Ignite Your Dream: The Quintessential Checklist for Aspiring Entrepreneurs" by Patrick H. Perrine is an immersive guide lighting the path towards entrepreneurial success.

This power-packed handbook propels you from dreaming to achieving with a carefully curated 100-step map. Dive into real-life entrepreneur stories, extract wisdom, and utilize actionable checklists. This book transcends theoretical guidelines, providing a mentorship experience designed to turn dreams into reality.

Ready to kindle your entrepreneurial spirit? "Ignite your Dream" is your step forward towards unlocking potential and achieving success in the exciting world of entrepreneurship.

Fail Fast, Recover Faster: Bouncing Back From Entrepreneurial Failure

Embrace failure and bounce back stronger with "Fail Fast, Recover Faster: Bouncing Back From Entrepreneurial Failure". It's your guidebook through the tumultuous journey of entrepreneurship, celebrating stumbles as stepping stones towards success.

Dive into compelling tales of triumphant entrepreneurs, learn how to pivot rapidly, manage fallout, and convert setbacks into launchpads. Discover strategies for repairing financial, relationship, and reputation damage, and see your failures as badges of resilience.

This transformative book readies you to rebound from failure swiftly, turning your setbacks into your next entrepreneurial triumph. With "Fail Fast, Recover Faster", you're poised to harness your own unicorn moment and turn failure into a launching pad for success.

Fueling the Fire: Nurturing Resilience and Preventing Burnout in Entrepreneurship

In "Fueling the Fire: Nurturing Resilience and Preventing Burnout in Entrepreneurship," seasoned entrepreneur Patrick H. Perrine guides you through the entrepreneurial journey, sharing practical strategies for maintaining resilience and passion.

Drawing from 20 years of startup experience, Perrine covers everything from ideation to acquisition. Discover how to build a support system, manage your time effectively, cultivate a positive work culture, and align your work with your values.

Whether you're an experienced entrepreneur or just beginning, "Fueling the Fire" is a must-read for maintaining balance and fulfillment in the dynamic world of entrepreneurship.